TACOS, TORTAS, AND TAMALES

TACOS, TORTAS, AND TAMALES

★★★★★★★★★

Flavors from the griddles, pots, and
streetside kitchens of Mexico

★★★

ROBERTO SANTIBAÑEZ

with JJ Goode

Photos by Todd Coleman

Designed by Memo Productions

Library of Congress Cataloging-in-Publication Data

Santibanez, Roberto.

Tacos, tortas, and tamales : flavors from the griddles, pots, and street-side kitchens of Mexico / Roberto Santibañez, JJ Goode, Todd Coleman.

    pages cm

ISBN 978-1-118-19020-3 (hardback); 978-1-118-28103-1 (ebk.); 978-1-118-28104-8 (ebk.); 978-1-118-28105-5 (ebk.)

1. Cooking, Mexican. I. Goode, J. J. II. Coleman, Todd, 1973- III. Title.

TX716.M4S2674 2012

641.5972--dc23

                                    2012006650

Printed in China

10   9   8   7   6   5   4   3   2   1

Cover and interior photography: © Todd Coleman

Cover and interior: Designed by Memo Productions

CONTENTS

Introduction

☆ ☆

AS YOU WALK THE STREETS OF MEXICO, you'd be forgiven for thinking that all we Mexicans do is eat. To your right is a cluster of makeshift stalls called *puestos*, smoke rising into the air smelling of charred beef and sizzling pork. You gawk as one vendor tucks salty bits of steak into tortillas and splashes on a little salsa, while another piles browned, juicy chorizo onto crusty rolls. Across the street, women preside over huge pots of *esquites*, a tremendously delicious snack of big starchy corn kernels cooked with epazote and topped with mayonnaise, cheese, and powdered chile—a trio almost as popular here as beans, rice, and tortillas. Others hawk slices of mango, cucumber, and jicama dressed up with salt, a good squeeze of lime, and, of course, plenty of chile. Then, WHOOSH! A bike rushes past carrying a basket of *tacos sudados*, a giant jar of salsa precariously attached to the basket by wire. Then you spin on your heels as a melancholy whistle sounds. It signals that the *camote* man has arrived with his pushcart, selling syrupy sweet potatoes and plantains drizzled with condensed milk. So evocative is the sound that my mom made it her cell phone ringtone.

It was in this food paradise that I grew up. I'd walk the bustling streets of Mexico City with my mom, hoping we would stop for a quesadilla or tamale on our way from somewhere to somewhere else—even occasionally on our way to dinner. Mexican food has developed a reputation for being complicated and inscrutable to outsiders, thanks in part to a few notorious moles, but the food of the street is often as simple as it is delicious.

Strange as it may sound, we Mexicans don't necessarily consider all of these treats to be "street food," as Americans do. Sure, there are some foods you more or less find only on the streets, but in Mexico, where so much of life takes place outdoors—in bustling squares, open-air markets, and restaurants whose seating spills onto the sidewalk—"the street" is a surprisingly expansive concept. Even tacos, the archetypal street food, are just as often enjoyed in proper restaurants as they are beside a man and his sidewalk griddle.

A better definition, then, might be "everyday food." It's food that Mexicans eat in one form or another every single day of our lives—the cinnamon-spiked strawberry smoothie I often make for breakfast or buy at the *licuado* stand, the slow-cooked lamb on tortillas that friends gobble down after work, the sandwiches made from leftover beans and cheese that our grandmothers make for lunch.

While working on my previous book, *Truly Mexican*, I found that limiting my scope (in that case, focusing on sauces) helped illuminate a cuisine that easily overwhelms outsiders with its awe-inspiring diversity. I also found that grouping similar dishes into families underscored the similarities, the techniques and ingredients that united the recipes. I applied the same logic here. I aimed my telescope at a particular culinary solar system and zoomed in on three constellations that are particularly close to my heart: tacos, tortas, and tamales. By focusing one chapter on *tortas*, the fantastic family of Mexican sandwiches, for instance, you take away not just recipes for classic

☆ ☆

tortas and the fundamental techniques that make them transcendent, but also the knowledge that nearly anything can become a torta and the skills to ensure your own creations are incredibly tasty.

While I've grouped these three items to accentuate that which unites them, you'll be struck by the incredible variety within each chapter. Remember, before Mexico was a unified country, the landmass was home to dozens of indigenous peoples, who even today retain their heritage through culture, language (dozens of distinct languages are spoken in modern Mexico), and, of course, the foods they eat. Even I occasionally forget the extent to which this defines contemporary cooking. I've eaten food cooked by two women who grew up in towns just minutes apart and was shocked to observe how different it was. I asked why, and it turns out that one of the women is Mixteca and the other is Zapoteca, two different indigenous groups. It is this diversity that makes Mexican food so endlessly fascinating, even for someone like me, who has spent decades studying it.

Besides the tacos, tortas, and tamales, I've also provided recipes for several other categories of everyday treats. There are salsas and condiments meant to enliven members of the main trio as well as your own daily meals. There is a colorful array of beverages, from the fresh fruit–filled *aguas frescas* and *licuados* that you'll find in Mexico's markets to the thick, warm drinks called *atoles,* ladled into cups from streetside pots, and even a few alcoholic treats that you'd sip from stools that spill onto squares. And finally, there are a bunch of unbelievably easy-to-make sweets, like one-pot coconut rice pudding, lime sorbet, Mexican-chocolate ice cream, and blend-and-serve mango cream with fresh berries. In general, the recipes in this book embrace the inherent simplicity that makes Mexican cooking magical, those dishes for which all you do is combine a handful of ingredients in the right way and suddenly, you have big, bold, brilliant flavor.

The casual nature of this food makes it particularly ripe for shortcuts and ingredient substitutions, so I offer them whenever you may apply them without forfeiting flavor. This is precisely what we do in Mexico, when our busy lives keep us from pressing our own tortillas or preparing mole from scratch. My hope is that this book will give you the tools to invent your own versions of these treats as well. For example, you'll love tamales filled with my short-cut mole, but perhaps you'll choose to fill yours instead with leftover rotisserie chicken and canned pickled jalapeños. There's no recipe in this book for papaya agua fresca or cheese and-avocado tortas, but after flipping through the respective chapters, you'll learn the simple tricks that apply to all aguas and tortas. Next thing you know, you've re-created the thrill of that corner in Mexico City or that market in Oaxaca right in your home kitchen.

☆ ☆

I'VE BEEN LUCKY ENOUGH TO WITNESS many taco revelations, the moments when visitors to Mexico bite into a taco that changes their lives. Perhaps it's the warm soft tortilla that does it. Maybe it's the little mound of tender steak or the streak of vibrant salsa. If I've picked the place, you can bet it's all three. What was once just a pleasant snack becomes a treat that you plan entire days around, one that you pine for as you lie in bed at night.

A taco, to put it simply, is anything eaten on a soft tortilla. From there, the possibilities are endless. For it's not just the incredible deliciousness that provides those revelations, it's also the seemingly infinite variety. There are taco spots that concentrate on familiar grilled meats and others that focus their energies on heaps of tender braised pork called carnitas, where your friendly counterman lets you select your ideal combination of pig parts—mine is the tender *espaldita* (meat from the lower back) with some *nanas* (the crunchy bits left in the pan).

Much to the surprise of my American friends, carnitas are a morning-to-early-afternoon taco filling, as is cow's head, the tender flesh of which is pulled from a pot with tongs. You're more likely to end a margarita-fueled night with *tacos al pastor*, the gorgeous hunks of marinated pork rotating on vertical spits. Some spots specialize in *tacos de guisado*, tortillas topped with a healthy spoonful of stews, moles, and other soupy creations. Vegetarians aren't left out, even in meat-loving Mexico. They feast on tacos filled with eggs and potatoes, strips of roasted poblano chiles called *rajas*, *quelites* (lovely, spinach-like wild greens), or sautéed mushrooms tinged with cream.

There are tacos specific to certain states in Mexico—slow-cooked achiote-marinated pork topped with pickled onions from the Yucatán, for one, and the fish tacos on flour tortillas common in Baja for another. The U.S. has contributed some delicious versions to the taco canon, including the Texan masterpiece known as the breakfast taco.

Yet for all the local specialties and time-tested combinations, the truth is that virtually anything can be taco fodder. Some cooks even fry the veins from the dried chiles and eat them inside a tortilla with salt. The result is a treat called *tacos de venas*. When I eat guacamole, I usually skip the chips that have become the standard accompaniment in the U.S. and do what I've done since I was a boy: wrap a tortilla around the soft, spicy chunks of avocado. Whether I'm eating chicken tinga, a simple stew made with tomato and chiles, or pot roast, if I have tortillas I'll make tacos.

These fillings tucked inside tortillas are just the half of it. Raising the ante is a boundless assortment of salsas and other toppings (page 121–149) that contribute fantastic jolts of salt, acidity, and spice. They're optional, but highly recommended. Lime wedges, too.

This chapter is dedicated to some of my favorite renditions of this Mexican treat. Some are classics, some are of my invention, but they're all fantastic!

Some of my favorite everyday tacos

☆ ☆ ☆

Warm tortillas + Store-bought rotisserie chicken + Mayonnaise + Chiles Toreados (page 145)

☆ ☆ ☆

Warm tortillas + Guacamole + Tomatillo-Chipotle Salsa (page 134)

☆ ☆ ☆

Warm tortillas + Cubes of queso fresco + Chiles Toreados (page 145)

☆ ☆ ☆

Warm tortillas + Eggs (scrambled, over easy, whatever you'd like) + Fresh Green Salsa (page 133)

☆ ☆

➜ HOW TO SERVE TACOS AT HOME: *Unless you're serving just two people, plating each taco yourself would be a full-time job that would have you chained to the stove all evening long. To save yourself the effort and to spare everyone soggy, cold tortillas, the best option is to set out a DIY feast: meat in warm pots; the salsas and garnishes in bowls; and a stack of warm tortillas in a basket or covered bowl.*

TORTILLAS

You can't have tacos without tortillas—the flat disks made from corn or, less frequently flour—which is their defining characteristic.

The corn used for tortillas is a starchy variety that's dried and soaked in hot water mixed with slaked lime. Known as nixtamalization, this soaking process alters the corn's chemical structure, unlocking nutrients and making the corn digestable. The result gets ground into a sort of dough called "masa." The highly perishable masa is either formed into tortillas and cooked briefly, or it's dried and powdered (this is the kind you'll see in supermarkets in Mexico and the U.S.), to be rehydrated with water. Flour tortillas, sometimes maligned as "inauthentic," are in fact a staple of the North of Mexico and as Mexican as I am. A mixture of lard and wheat flour, both of which became available after the conquest, well-made flour tortillas are incredibly delicate and delicious.

"Tortilla" is a Spanish word that the early visitors to Mexico used for the disks of corn dough that the indigenous people ate, probably so called because the newcomers thought these disks resembled the shape of the omelet-like egg-and-potato "tortillas" of Spain. Before the time of the conquest, indigenous folks called what they were eating by the Nahuatl word "*tlaxcala*." In the distant past, these were large, much like the dinner-plate-sized *tlayudas* you find today on the streets of Oaxaca, and heftier than the thin ones to which we've all become accustomed.

ADVANCED TACO-MAKING

You can serve fantastic tacos with store-bought tortillas (see page 13), but homemade tortillas make great tacos even better. Fresh masa is wonderful if you can find it—depending on where you live, this can be pretty easy or really difficult. Since it doesn't travel well, you can't order it online. Fortunately, tortilla flour makes a solid substitute and is easy to find.

STORING TORTILLAS

Wrap tortillas you don't use in a kitchen towel, then store them in an airtight plastic bag in the fridge. Store-bought tortillas last for a week or so in the fridge; homemade tortillas last up to three days.

CORN TORTILLAS
Tortillas de maíz

☆ ☆

3 cups tortilla flour (masa harina)

¾ teaspoon kosher salt

2½ cups warm water (about 115°F), plus more as needed

EQUIPMENT

Tortilla press (see opposite page)

Two plastic rounds (about 7 inches in diameter) cut from a thin, translucent grocery bag with the tip of a sharp knife

→ **MAKES 24 TORTILLAS** ★

Please don't be put off by the detailed instructions. They're meant to ensure that your first few tortilla-making sessions go swimmingly. Once you get the hang of the process, you'll see how simple and satisfying it is, and I hope thereafter you'll need no more than a peek at my instructions.

MAKE THE DOUGH:

★ Stir together the tortilla flour and salt in a large bowl. Add the water and mix with your hands until the mixture comes together, then knead it for a minute with your palm to form a smooth dough. It should feel just slightly sticky and leave a light film on your hands. If it doesn't, very gradually knead in more water until it does. Put the dough back in the bowl, cover it with plastic wrap, and let it sit for 5 minutes or up to 2 hours.

FORM AND COOK THE TORTILLAS:

★ Set a large shallow (ideally, flat) pan over medium-high heat until it begins to smoke. Line a tortilla basket or a bowl with a clean kitchen towel: As you cook each tortilla, you will layer it on top of the others in the basket, wrap the basket with the towel, and cover it (with an inverted plate in the case of the bowl) to finish cooking the tortillas and to keep them warm.

★ Open your tortilla press and lay a plastic round in the center of the press's bottom plate. Grab a small piece of dough (about 2 tablespoons' worth) and roll it between your palms into a ball. Put it in the center of the plastic round, drape the other plastic round on top, and press down gently with your palm to flatten the ball a bit. Close the tortilla press, push down firmly on the handle, open the press again, rotate the plastic rounds 180 degrees, and press down again. Your goal is a tortilla of even thickness.

★ Open the press, pick up the tortilla, plastic and all, and carefully peel off the plastic from one side and then the other. (If the tortilla sticks to the plastic, the dough is too wet and you should gradually add a little more tortilla flour.) With the tortilla draped on your palm, gently lay the tortilla (resist the temptation to flop it) onto the pan with a turn of your wrist.

★ Set a timer if it's your first or even third time cooking tortillas. Cook the tortilla on one side until the edges just barely lift from the pan, about 20 seconds. Use your fingers or a spatula to carefully flip the tortilla, then cook it for 45 seconds. Flip it again, cook it for 45 seconds (it should puff slightly), then flip it one final time, and cook for 30 seconds. Each side should have a few brown spots. (If there are no brown spots, the heat is too low. If the spots look dark, the heat is too high.)

★ Put the cooked tortilla in the kitchen towel–lined basket or bowl, cover, and one by one, repeat forming and cooking the tortillas.

➤ **TORTILLA PRESS:** *Corn tortillas require a tortilla press. Flimsy, cheap ones never do the job as well as heavy wooden, cast-iron, or cast-aluminum ones. A good press will cost anywhere from $25 to $60, and it'll be worth every penny. One readily available and relatively inexpensive press is the one from Imusa with the word "Victoria" printed on its top. (imusausa.com)*

➤ **THE JOY OF A WARM TORTILLA:** *Even if you don't make tortillas yourself, you can have fantastic tacos as long as you make sure store-bought tortillas are properly warmed. Here's how to do it:*

- *Heat a pan over moderately high heat until just before it begins to smoke.*
- *Meanwhile, line a tortilla basket or large bowl with a clean kitchen towel.*
- *Cook the tortillas one or two at a time, flipping them frequently, until they're warm and pliable, but stopping before they get brittle or dried out, about 1½ minutes for corn tortillas and 45 seconds for flour tortillas.*
- *Stack each one in the kitchen towel-lined container, wrap it in the towel, and cover the basket while you heat the rest. They'll keep warm for about 30 minutes.*

FLOUR TORTILLAS
Tortillas de harina

☆ ☆

1⅓ cups warm water (about 115°F)

1 tablespoon plus 2 teaspoons kosher salt

½ cup plus 2 tablespoons safflower or vegetable oil

4½ cups unbleached bread flour (from a 2-pound bag), plus extra for dusting

⅛ teaspoon baking powder

½ teaspoon sugar

EQUIPMENT:
Stand mixer with a dough hook attachment

A small rolling pin

→ **MAKES ABOUT 30 TORTILLAS ★**

Often mistaken for a Tex-Mex invention, flour tortillas have a long history in Mexico. They're particularly beloved by those from the North of the country, but you'll find them in cities far and wide. While they're typically made with lard, I find it's easier to use safflower oil in the U.S., and the result is just as lovely.

MAKE THE DOUGH:

★ Combine the water and salt in the bowl of the stand mixer and whisk until the salt dissolves, then whisk in the oil. In a separate bowl, stir together the flour, baking powder, and sugar. Use a rubber spatula to stir the flour mixture into the oil mixture until you have a dry-looking dough.

★ Attach the dough hook and mix the dough on the lowest speed for 2 minutes. Increase the speed by a notch and mix for 1 minute, then increase the speed by another notch and mix for 2 minutes more. You'll have a slightly sticky, very elastic dough.

★ Remove the dough from the mixer and use your hands to knead it for a few seconds on a lightly floured work surface, then form a smooth ball. Cover the dough with a kitchen towel or plastic wrap and let it rest for 10 minutes.

★ Divide the dough into about 30 equal-sized pieces, each a little smaller than a Ping Pong ball (or 1 ounce, if you have a scale). Cover the dough pieces again.

★ Use your palm to "round" each piece of dough: cup your palm over the dough, then apply light pressure to roll the dough into a ball, keeping your fingertips and the heel of your palm parallel to the work surface.

FORM AND COOK THE TORTILLAS:

★ Working with one at a time, put a ball of dough on a floured surface, flatten it with the palm of your hand, then lightly flour the top of the dough. Use a small rolling pin to create an even, very thin (the thinner the better) disk about 6½ inches in diameter, rolling back and forth then rotating the dough a quarter turn until you have a disk of even thickness.

★ Set a large shallow (ideally, flat) pan over medium-high heat and let it get good and hot. Line a tortilla basket or a bowl with a clean kitchen towel: As you cook each tortilla, you will layer it on top of the others in the basket, wrap the basket with the towel, and cover it (with an inverted plate in the case of the bowl) to keep the tortillas moist and warm.

★ Carefully lay the tortilla flat onto the pan. Cook until the edges begin to lift from the pan and the bottom has developed a few golden spots (dark spots mean the heat is too high), about 30 seconds. Flip with a spatula, cook for 30 seconds, then flip again and cook until it puffs, 20 seconds more, pressing down with the spatula to keep it flat. Keep cooking, flipping every few seconds, until there are golden brown spots on both sides, about 10 seconds more.

★ Put the cooked tortilla in the kitchen towel-lined basket or bowl, cover, and continue rolling and then cooking each ball.

TACOS OF ROASTED POBLANOS AND CREAM
Tacos de rajas con crema

☆ ☆

FOR THE RAJAS:

1¼ pounds fresh poblano chiles (about 3 large)

Generous 1 tablespoon olive or vegetable oil

½ medium white onion, thinly sliced into half-moons

½ teaspoon kosher salt

Generous ⅛ teaspoon black pepper

1 medium garlic clove, finely chopped

½ cup Mexican crema or crème fraîche

Generous 1 tablespoon finely chopped epazote leaves, or ½ teaspoon dried Mexican oregano

→ **MAKES 8 TACOS** ★

Rajas, meaty strips of roasted chiles, make excellent vegetarian tacos, and this classic version is as rich and satisfying as any pile of pork. All that richness craves a little spice, so if your poblanos have no heat (some pack a tingle, to be sure), don't neglect the black pepper in the recipe or be sure to spoon on spicy salsa before serving.

★ Turn two stove-top burners to high and roast the poblano chiles on the racks of the burners (or directly on the element of an electric stove), turning frequently with tongs, until they are blistered and charred all over, 4 to 6 minutes. Put the poblanos in a bowl and cover with a plate to sweat for 15 to 20 minutes.

★ Rub off the skin from the roasted poblanos with a paper towel or your fingers (do not run the poblanos under water), then cut them open lengthwise. Cut out the stems, seed pods, and veins, and lay the chiles flat. Wipe the chiles clean of seeds, discard the seeds, and slice the chiles into long ¼-inch-thick strips.

★ Heat the oil in a medium pan over medium heat until the oil shimmers, then add the onion, ¼ teaspoon of the salt, and the pepper, and cook until the onion is soft and translucent, about 5 minutes. Add the garlic, cook for a minute, then add the poblanos along with the remaining ¼ teaspoon of salt. Cook for 3 minutes or so, then add the crema and epazote.

★ Let it come to a simmer and cook, stirring, until the crema thickens slightly and coats the poblanos, about 3 minutes. Season to taste with salt.

★ Serve alongside **8 WARM CORN TORTILLAS** and top with **CRUMBLED QUESO FRESCO** and **FRIED CHILE SALSA** (page 138) or **SMOKY TOMATO SALSA** (page 130).

→ *Rajas with cream also makes a fantastic meal spooned over white rice. Try it with a cup of sweet corn kernels added along with the onions.*

MUSHROOM TACOS
Tacos de hongos

☆ ☆

FOR THE MUSHROOMS:

¼ generous cup olive or vegetable oil

Generous 1 cup diced white onions

3 fresh serrano or jalapeño chiles, finely chopped (including seeds)

3 medium garlic cloves, finely chopped

1¼ pounds fresh mushrooms, stems trimmed, cut into 1-inch pieces

1½ teaspoons kosher salt

2 tablespoons unsalted butter

1 tablespoon finely chopped fresh epazote leaves, or ¼ cup chopped cilantro

⋯⋯⋯⋯⋯⋯⋯⋯⋯⋯⋯⋯⋯⋯

→ MAKES 10 TACOS ★

⋯⋯⋯⋯⋯⋯⋯⋯⋯⋯⋯⋯⋯⋯

A little effort, a lot of flavor. Multiple varieties of mushrooms (try cremini, oyster, and shiitake) make for an even more exciting combination of textures, but even plain old portobellos become something special with the addition of chile, herbs, and a touch of butter. Without the tortillas and condiments, you have a side dish that goes well with just about any taco or tamale you can dream up.

★ Heat the oil in a large heavy pan over high heat. When it shimmers, add the onions, chiles, and garlic and cook, stirring frequently, until the onions are translucent, about 2 minutes.

★ Add the mushrooms, toss very well to coat in the oil, and cook, stirring occasionally, until the mushrooms are cooked through and lightly browned, 12 to 15 minutes. Add the salt and cook for 2 minutes more, then stir in the butter and epazote until the butter has melted. Season to taste with salt.

★ Serve alongside 10 WARM CORN TORTILLAS and top with CRUMBLED QUESO FRESCO and SLICED CANNED PICKLED JALAPEÑO CHILES or TOMATILLO-CHIPOTLE SALSA (page 134), FRESH GUAJE SALSA (page 142), or HABANERO AND BELL PEPPER SALSA WITH CREAM (page 131).

TACOS OF POTATOES IN GREEN SALSA
Tacos de papas en salsa verde

☆ ☆

A must-try for vegetarians and carnivores alike, this meatless taco is a staple at places selling tacos de guisado. Tart tomatillo sauce coats crispy potatoes, and a last-minute dose of cheese makes for a magnificently messy meal, whether the potatoes fill tacos or stand in for the hash browns that accompany your next breakfast.

FOR THE POTATOES:

1 pound fingerling, red-skinned, or Yukon Gold potatoes

Kosher salt

¼ cup canola oil

1½ cups Boiled Tomatillo Salsa (see page 23)

5 ounces Chihuahua or provolone cheese, shredded

½ cup chopped cilantro

→ **MAKES 12 TACOS** ★

★ Put the potatoes in a medium pot and add enough cold water to cover them by one inch. Salt the water generously. Set the pot over high heat, let the water come to a boil, then lower the heat to medium and cook at a simmer just until the potatoes are fork-tender, 12 to 18 minutes, depending on the size of the potatoes. Drain the potatoes. When they're cool enough to handle, cut the potatoes into 1-inch chunks.

★ Pour the oil into a sauté pan that's just large enough to hold the potatoes in one layer and set the pan over high heat. When it's very hot (test by adding one potato chunk; the oil should immediately bubble rapidly), carefully add the potatoes to the oil. Cook without stirring until the potatoes are deep golden brown on one side, about 3 minutes. Continue cooking, turning the potatoes occasionally so each side gets color, until they're deep golden brown all over, about 8 minutes, transferring them to a plate once they're done.

★ Drain the oil, return the potatoes to the pan, and add the salsa. Let it come to a boil, then lower the heat to maintain a steady simmer and cook, stirring and breaking up some of the potatoes, about 5 minutes.

★ Add the cheese to the hot potato mixture, remove the pan from the heat, and stir until the cheese has completely melted. Stir in the cilantro.

★ Serve alongside **12 WARM CORN TORTILLAS** and top with additional **CHOPPED CILANTRO**.

BOCADILLOS:
- Gialdritas
- Medias Noches
- Volovanes
- Teleritas
- Marinas
- Empanadilas
- Pambacitos
- Preparados o Vacios

Pedido Minimo por Clase 50 Piezas

El Chef guevara
Choripan $37
Pesetto $413
Provoleta $45
Salchicha $37
Parrillera $37
Queso Extra $8"

BOILED TOMATILLO SALSA

Salsa verde cocida

★ ★

★ Combine the tomatillos and chiles in a medium pot, add enough water to cover them, and bring the water to a simmer over high heat. Lower the heat to maintain a gentle simmer and cook until the tomatillos turn khaki green and are soft but still intact, about 15 minutes. Drain gently, then blend the tomatillos and chiles with the onion, garlic, and salt until very smooth, at least a minute.

★ Heat the oil in a small pot or saucepan over medium heat until it shimmers. Add the salsa and simmer, stirring frequently, until slightly thickened, about 15 minutes. Season to taste with salt.

★ **MAKE AHEAD:** The salsa keeps in the fridge for up to three days.

1 pound tomatillos (10 to 12), husked and rinsed

2 fresh serrano or jalapeño chiles, stemmed

¼ cup roughly chopped white onion

2 medium garlic cloves, peeled

1 teaspoon kosher salt

1 tablespoon olive or vegetable oil

→ **MAKES 2 CUPS** ★

CACTUS TACOS
Tacos de nopales

☆ ☆

FOR THE CACTUS:

2 pounds young cactus paddles (about 12 thin), trimmed and sliced (see note, below)

1 cup finely chopped white onions

5 medium garlic cloves, peeled

Generous 1 tablespoon dried Mexican oregano

3 dried chiles de árbol, wiped clean (optional)

2 tablespoons olive or vegetable oil

2 teaspoons kosher salt

······································

→ MAKES 12 TACOS ★

······································

My grandmother made the best *nopales*. Her cactus strips always had a soft crunch and lovely slick texture, a little like that of cooked shiitake mushrooms. One thing they were not was *baboso*, or "slimy." Her secret was in her cooking method, which is a bit like that for cooking carnitas: You simmer the cactus in water and a little oil until the water evaporates and the cactus cooks further in the sizzling oil, which she said eradicates the *baba*.

★ Combine the cactus, onions, garlic, oregano, chiles, oil, and salt in a sauté pan (approximately 12 inches in diameter). Add 1 cup of water and bring to a boil over medium-high heat. Cook at a vigorous simmer, stirring occasionally, until the water has evaporated, about 25 minutes.

★ Continue cooking in the oil remaining in the pan, stirring often, until the cactus is very lightly browned, about 5 minutes. Remove the garlic cloves. Season to taste with salt.

★ MAKE AHEAD: Covered and refrigerated, the cactus keeps for up to two days.

★ Serve alongside **12 WARM CORN TORTILLAS** and top with **CRUMBLED QUESO FRESCO** or **GOAT CHEESE** and **FRIED CHILE SALSA** (page 138) or **FRESH GUAJE SALSA** (page 142).

→ BUYING AND PREPPING CACTUS: *Buy the smallest, thinnest paddles you can find, because these young paddles will be more tender than older, larger paddles.*

If the paddles haven't already been trimmed of thorns (be careful not to prick yourself when handling cactus!), use a sharp knife held parallel to the paddles to trim the thorns from both sides and trim the border of each paddle. Rinse the paddles and drain well.

To slice them before cooking, find the thick part of each paddle and cut it off. Slice the thin part into 2 × ¼-inch batons, then slice the thick part into 2 × ⅛-inch batons.

→ You can also make tortas from nopales, each roll spread with black beans and the cactus topped with queso fresco and pico de gallo. Cactus is also lovely scrambled with eggs.

SHRIMP TACOS

Tacos de camarón

☆ ☆

FOR THE SHRIMP:

1½ pounds peeled deveined medium shrimp (about 60)

2 heaping tablespoons finely chopped garlic

1 tablespoon plus 1 teaspoon freshly squeezed lime juice

2 teaspoons Worcestershire sauce

1 teaspoon dried oregano, preferably Mexican

1 teaspoon kosher salt

1 teaspoon freshly ground black pepper

About 2 tablespoons extra-virgin olive oil

→ MAKES 16 TACOS ★

To channel the flavors you'd find in coastal northern Mexico, I turn to a simple flash-marinade that electrifies shrimp. Add the crunch of cabbage and just about any salsa you like and you have tasty, light tacos easy enough for a weeknight dinner. My advice: Serve these with tartar sauce *and* salsa.

PREPARE THE SHRIMP:

★ Combine the shrimp, garlic, lime juice, Worcestershire, oregano, salt, pepper, and 1 tablespoon of the olive oil in a large bowl, and toss well.

★ Heat a large pan over high heat and add just enough olive oil to create a thin film on the bottom of the pan. Working in several batches to avoid crowding the pan, cook the shrimp until they are lightly browned and just cooked through, turning the shrimp over halfway through, about 30 seconds per side. Let the pan get hot again before cooking each batch. Season to taste with salt.

★ Serve alongside **16 WARM CORN OR FLOUR TORTILLAS** and top with **HABANERO SALSA WITH CREAM** (page 131) or **SHREDDED CABBAGE, MEXICAN TARTAR SAUCE** (page 149) and **PICO DE GALLO WITH LEMON ZEST** (page 127).

TACO OF POBLANOS AND BACON
Tacos de rajas con tocino

☆☆☆☆☆☆☆☆☆☆☆☆☆☆☆☆☆☆☆☆☆☆☆☆☆☆☆☆☆△△△

Crispy bits of bacon and a web of melty cheese unite strips of roasted poblano chiles in this incredible mixture that needs no salsa or topping. That said, tomato salsa certainly wouldn't hurt and, if you really want a rich treat, stir in cheese until it melts.

〰〰〰〰〰〰〰〰〰〰〰〰〰〰〰〰〰〰〰

PREPARE THE RAJAS:

★ Roast, peel, seed, and cut the poblanos as described on page 16.

★ Meanwhile, heat a large pan over medium-high heat, add the bacon and cook, stirring occasionally and lowering the heat slightly once the bacon renders its fat, until the bacon is uniformly golden brown and slightly crisp, about 8 minutes.

★ Discard all but 2 tablespoons of the fat, then add the onion to the pan. Cook the onion, stirring, until soft and translucent, about 5 minutes. Add the garlic and pepper and cook 1 minute, then add the poblanos, salt, and Worcestershire sauce. Cook until the poblanos are warmed through, about 3 minutes.

★ Add the cheese, turn off the heat, and toss until the cheese is melted.

★ Taste and season with salt, if necessary, since bacon varies in saltiness.

★ Serve alongside **10 WARM CORN TORTILLAS** and top with **SMOKY TOMATO SALSA** (page 130).

FOR THE RAJAS:

1¼ pounds fresh poblano chiles (about 3 large)

6 thick-cut slices bacon (about 6 ounces), coarsely chopped

1 medium white onion, thinly sliced into half-moons

1 medium garlic clove, finely chopped

⅛ teaspoon freshly ground black pepper

¼ teaspoon kosher salt

Generous ½ teaspoon Worcestershire sauce

¼ pound Chihuahua or provolone cheese, shredded (optional)

┈┈┈┈┈┈┈┈┈┈┈┈┈┈┈┈

→ MAKES 10 TACOS ★

┈┈┈┈┈┈┈┈┈┈┈┈┈┈┈┈

FISH TACOS
Tacos de pescado

☆ ☆

FOR THE FISH:

About 16 saltines

1 large egg

¾ teaspoon kosher salt

½ teaspoon freshly ground black pepper

½ teaspoon dried Mexican oregano

1 pound skinless boneless cod, flounder, or tilapia fillets, cut into ¾-inch chunks

Canola or vegetable oil for frying

··
→ **MAKES 12 TACOS** ★
··

It's easy to see why fish tacos have become as popular in the U.S. as tongue tacos are south of the border. A warm tortilla, the soft crunch of cabbage, and moist fish encased in a crisp coating—what could be better? Well, add a healthy squeeze of lime, my pickled jalapeño–spiked tartar sauce, and pico de gallo and you have your answer.

★ Pulse the saltines in a blender (or add them to a resealable plastic bag and use your hands to smash them) until you have a mixture of fine and slightly coarse crumbs. Put 1 cup of them in a large bowl.

★ Crack the egg into a medium bowl. Add the salt, pepper, and oregano, and beat well. Add the fish to the egg mixture and toss well to coat. Use your hands to lift the fish from the egg mixture, letting any excess egg mixture drip back into the bowl, then add the fish to the crumbs and toss with your hands, pressing the fish gently to make sure each piece is well coated in crumbs. Transfer the breaded fish to a plate.

★ Pour 3 inches of oil into a Dutch oven or medium pot and heat the oil over medium-high heat until it reaches 375°F on a deep-fry thermometer. Working in batches to avoid crowding the oil, fry the fish until the outside is golden brown, about 2 minutes per batch. Drain on paper towels.

★ Serve alongside **12 WARM CORN TORTILLAS** and top with **SHREDDED CABBAGE** or **ROMAINE LETTUCE, MEXICAN TARTAR SAUCE** (page 149), and **PICO DE GALLO WITH LEMON ZEST** (page 127).

CHOPPED FRIED-FISH TACOS
Tacos de salpicón de pescado

☆ ☆

Take fried fish, break it up, and douse it with lime juice, Worcestershire sauce, chiles, and cilantro, and you have an incredible jumble of textures and flavors. Because you hack the fish into bits, there's no need to find perfect-for-presentation fillets, so this is a great way to use those that aren't flawless, as long as they're fresh.

★ Put the fish in a large bowl, add 1 tablespoon of the lime juice and the salt, and toss well. Put the frying flour in another large bowl, add the fish, and toss very well to evenly coat the fish.

★ Pour 3 inches of canola oil into a Dutch oven or medium pot and heat the oil over medium-high heat until it reaches 375°F on a deep-fry thermometer. Working in batches to avoid crowding the oil, shake off a little flour from the fish, then add the fish to the oil and fry until the pieces are lightly golden brown and crispy, about 2 minutes per batch. Transfer the fried fish to a paper towel to drain.

★ When the fish is just cool enough to handle, put it in a large bowl and add the onions, cilantro, chiles, Worcestershire sauce, olive oil, and the remaining 2 tablespoons of lime juice. Toss and mix well with your hands or a spoon, breaking up the strips into small pieces as you do. Season to taste with more lime juice, chiles, and salt.

★ Serve alongside **16 WARM CORN TORTILLAS** and **LIME WEDGES** and top with slices of **RIPE MEXICAN HASS AVOCADO** or **CREMA** and **FRESH GREEN SALSA** (page 133).

FOR THE FISH:

1 pound skinless boneless cod, flounder, or tilapia fillets, cut into approximately 3×½-inch strips

3 tablespoons freshly squeezed lime juice, plus more to taste

1 teaspoon kosher salt

1 recipe Frying Flour (page 50)

Canola or vegetable oil for frying

1 cup finely diced white onions

1 cup chopped cilantro

2 fresh serrano or jalapeño chiles, finely chopped (including seeds), plus more to taste

5 teaspoons Worcestershire sauce

2 tablespoons extra-virgin olive or vegetable oil

→ **MAKES 16 TACOS** ★

ADOBO-MARINATED CHICKEN TACOS
Tacos de pollo asado en adobo

☆ ☆

FOR THE CHICKEN:

4 dried guajillo chiles (about 1 ounce), wiped clean, stemmed, slit open, seeded, and deveined

4 dried ancho chiles (about 2 ounces), wiped clean, stemmed, slit open, seeded, and deveined

2 teaspoons chopped peeled ginger

¾ teaspoon ground cumin

¼ teaspoon freshly ground black pepper

1½ teaspoons kosher salt

2 pounds chicken cutlets

About 2 tablespoons olive or vegetable oil

....
→ **MAKES 16 TACOS ★**
....

A four-ingredient chile puree (no toasting required) ignites chicken breasts, turning the typically boring white meat into taco heaven. You'll have more than you'll need for this recipe, which is just fine, since it keeps in the fridge for up to five days and in the freezer for a couple of months.

★ Combine the chiles in a large bowl and add enough water to cover them. Soak the chiles until they're soft, about 30 minutes. Drain and discard the soaking water.

★ Blend the soaked chiles with the ginger, cumin, pepper, salt, and ½ cup of fresh water in a blender until the mixture is very smooth. You'll probably have to poke and pulse to help it blend. Don't be tempted to add more water, because you want the puree to be as thick as possible.

★ Put the chicken in a bowl, add ½ cup of the chile puree (reserving the rest for another purpose), and rub it onto the chicken until the meat is well coated. Cook right away, or even better, marinate for up to a few hours.

★ Preheat a grill, griddle, or large skillet over medium heat. Add just enough oil to add a thin sheen to the grill grates or pan. Season the chile-slathered breasts with salt and cook, in batches if necessary, until they're well browned on both sides and just cooked through, turning them over once, 8 to 10 minutes per batch. Let the chicken rest for a few minutes, then slice or dice it for tacos.

★ Serve alongside **16 WARM CORN TORTILLAS** and **LIME WEDGES** and top with **ANGRY CHILES** (page 145) or **FINELY CHOPPED WHITE ONION, CHOPPED CILANTRO**, and **ROASTED CHERRY TOMATO SALSA** (page 126) or **FRESH GREEN SALSA WITH AVOCADO** (page 133).

DUCK CARNITAS TACOS
Tacos de carnitas de pato

☆ ★ ★ ⬠ ⬠

Since you can make tacos of virtually anything, it's only natural that something as flavorful as duck would become a common sight on higher-end menus in the U.S. and Mexico. And just wait until you try this easy version! You make what amounts to a no-effort Mexican duck confit—as the duck bakes, its fat slowly renders and by the time the meat is tender, the duck has been treated to a gentle bath in its own fat infused with the aroma of Mexican cinnamon and orange. Shred the meat, crisp it in a pan, and your guests will be very happy indeed.

FOR THE DUCK:

4½ pounds duck legs (about 4 large legs or 6 smaller legs)

2 medium white onions, sliced

1 medium garlic head, halved horizontally

1 (5-inch) stick Mexican cinnamon, broken into a few pieces

2 tablespoons kosher salt

1 medium orange, quartered

2 tablespoons reserved duck fat or canola oil

→ MAKES 12 TACOS ★

★ Preheat the oven to 350°F. In a 6- to 8-quart Dutch oven or ovenproof pot, combine the duck legs, onions, garlic, cinnamon, and salt. Squeeze the orange quarters over the duck and add the spent oranges to the pot. Toss gently with your hands, arranging the duck legs skin side up.

★ Cover and cook the duck, shuffling the positions of the duck legs once, until the meat comes easily off the bone with a twist of a fork, about 2½ hours.

★ Remove the duck from the liquid fat in the pot, let it cool slightly, and pull the meat into large chunks, discarding the skin and bones. You should have about 3 cups of meat. Strain the duck fat through a sieve. Heat 2 tablespoons of the duck fat in a large pan over medium heat. Work in batches, if necessary, to avoid crowding the pan. Cook the duck, stirring occasionally, until the meat is golden brown and slightly crisp in spots, about 3 minutes. Season to taste with salt.

★ Serve alongside **12 WARM CORN TORTILLAS** and top with **FINELY CHOPPED WHITE ONION, CHOPPED CILANTRO,** and **JALAPENO AND PINEAPPLE SALSA** (page 137) or **TOMATILLO-CHIPOTLE SALSA** (page 134).

→ *Let the remaining fat cool fully and scrape off and reserve the delicious jellied liquid from the bottom. Scrape off and discard anything that isn't white. Store the fat, covered, in the fridge for up to three weeks or in the freezer for up to two months.*

TACOS with TOMATO-CHIPOTLE DUCK STEW
Tacos de tinga de pato

☆ △ △

This treatment of tender shredded duck ups the ante on the already delicious tortilla-topper, coating the meat in a smoky sauce that brings out its sweetness. Served in a heap right from the pot, it makes a great make-ahead taco showpiece. It also makes a fine filling for tamales or for a simple sandwich, like a luxe version of pulled pork.

★ Heat the duck fat or canola oil in a medium-large pan over medium-high heat. Add the onions, chile, bay leaf, thyme, and a generous pinch of the salt. Cook, stirring occasionally, until the onion is translucent, about 3 minutes. Add the tomatoes, garlic, the remaining salt, and the sugar (only if your tomatoes aren't that sweet), and cook, stirring frequently, until the tomatoes begin to break down and any liquid in the pan has almost completely evaporated, about 10 minutes.

★ Add the duck liquid, stock, or water and simmer for 2 minutes. Add the duck meat and simmer, stirring and breaking up the chunks of duck, until the meat is heated through and the flavors have melded, about 10 minutes.

★ MAKE AHEAD: The mixture keeps for up to three days in the fridge. Reheat it gently over low heat.

★ Serve alongside **12 WARM CORN TORTILLAS** and top with **SLICED CANNED PICKLED JALAPEÑO CHILES** and **CREMA** or **HABANERO SALSA WITH CREAM** (page 131).

FOR THE STEW:

1 tablespoon reserved duck fat or canola oil (page 33)

¾ cup diced white onion

1 dried chipotle mora chile (small, purplish-red), wiped clean and finely chopped

1 dried bay leaf

¼ teaspoon dried thyme

½ teaspoon kosher salt

1½ cups diced tomatoes (from about 1 large)

1 large garlic clove, finely chopped

½ teaspoon sugar, if necessary

½ cup reserved duck cooking liquid (page 33), chicken stock, or water

3 cups shredded duck meat (page 33)

→ MAKES 12 TACOS ★

DUCK TACOS IN HABANERO CREAM SAUCE
Tacos de pato salceados

☆ ☆

About 6 tablespoons mild
  olive or vegetable oil

12 corn tortillas

Tomato-Chipotle Duck Stew
  (page 35), warm

About 3 cups Habanero
  Salsa with Cream
  (page 131)

....
→ **MAKES 12 TACOS** ★
....

This unforgettable dish toes the line between taco and enchilada to thrilling effect. Silky, tongue-tickling cream-spiked habanero salsa blankets tortillas rolled around sweet and smoky shredded duck.

★ Preheat the oven to 300°F.

★ Heat 2 tablespoons of the oil in a small skillet (just large enough to fit a tortilla) over medium heat until it shimmers. One by one, cook the tortillas in the oil (the oil should be hot enough so that it sizzles around the edges of the tortilla), adding more oil as necessary, and letting it get hot, for 10 seconds per side. Use tongs to transfer each tortilla to two layers of paper towels to drain.

★ Put about ¼ cup of the duck stew on a tortilla, roll it up, transfer it, seam side down, to a baking pan, and repeat with the remaining tortillas and duck stew. Bake in the oven just until the tortillas and filling are hot, about 10 minutes.

★ Meanwhile, in a small saucepan, heat the salsa along with a splash of water over low heat until it comes to a bare simmer.

★ Divide the tacos among plates (or keep them in the baking dish) and spoon the warm salsa generously over them. Serve right away.

→ **CRISPY PASILLA CHILE GARNISH (optional):** *Wipe 4 dried pasillas clean with a damp paper towel and use scissors to cut the chiles into small pieces; discard the seeds that fall out. Heat ½ inch of oil in a skillet until it shimmers, add the pasilla pieces, and cook just until they crisp, about 30 seconds. Transfer them to a paper towel with a slotted spoon.*

POTATO AND CHORIZO TACOS
Tacos de papas con chorizo

☆ ☆ ☆ ☆ ☆ ☆ ☆ ☆ ☆ ☆ ☆ ☆ ☆ ☆ ☆ ☆ ☆ ★ ▲ ☆ ☆ ☆ ☆ ☆ ☆ ☆ ☆ ☆ ☆ ☆ ☆ ☆ ☆ ☆

A common sight in Mexico, chorizo sausage infuses potatoes with its salty, spicy flavor for a hearty taco filler.

★ Put the potatoes in a small pot and add enough cold water to cover them. Salt the water generously, and bring the water to a boil over high heat. Lower the heat and cook at a vigorous simmer until the potatoes are tender, 10 to 15 minutes, depending on the size of your potatoes. Drain the potatoes, and when they're cool enough to handle, remove the peel with your fingers as best you can and cut the potatoes into ½-inch cubes.

★ Put the chorizo in a cold, large, heavy pan or cast-iron skillet and set it over medium-high heat. Cook, stirring and breaking up the chorizo slightly, until it's completely cooked and lightly browned, about 15 minutes. Add the onions and chile, along with a teaspoon or two of oil if your chorizo hasn't rendered much fat, and cook, stirring and scraping, until the onions are translucent and soft, about 8 minutes.

★ Add the potatoes and ¼ teaspoon of salt, and cook until the potatoes are hot all the way through and have absorbed some chorizo flavor, about 10 minutes. As you cook, mash some of the potatoes. Season with salt to taste.

★ Serve alongside **12 WARM CORN TORTILLAS** and top with **CREMA, CHOPPED CILANTRO**, and **FRESH GREEN SALSA** (page 133) or **TOMATILLO-ÁRBOL SALSA** (page 134).

FOR THE FILLING:

1 pound red-skinned or Yukon Gold potatoes

Kosher salt

¾ pound Mexican chorizo, casings removed, if necessary

1 cup finely chopped white onions

1 tablespoon finely chopped fresh serrano or jalapeño chile (including seeds)

About 2 teaspoons olive or vegetable oil, if necessary

→ **MAKES 12 TACOS** ★

CARNITAS (SLOW-COOKED PORK) TACOS
Tacos de carnitas

☆ ☆

FOR THE CARNITAS:

8 medium garlic cloves, peeled

½ medium white onion, roughly chopped

1 tablespoon dried Mexican oregano

½ teaspoon dried thyme

5 teaspoons kosher salt

5 pounds boneless pork shoulder, cut into 2-inch chunks

3 dried bay leaves

1 cup Coca-Cola

→ **MAKES 24 TACOS ★**

Restaurants and stands throughout Mexico, especially in Michoacán, Mexico City, and Guanajuato, specialize in this pork-lover's fantasy, meat simmered until the liquid evaporates and all that's left is fat. This fat then fries the pork, giving the pieces savory, crisp edges. To make it, many cooks in my home country put an entire pig, butchered into parts, in a giant copper pot to bubble away and customers order by calling out their favorites, perhaps the *cueritos* (soft, sticky bits of skin), *pierna* (leg), or even *surtida* (a mixture of different parts). Because I suspect you might not have an enormous copper pot in your cupboard—I know I don't!—I've come up with an incredibly easy way to recreate the flavors of true *carnitas* with the help of my Guanajuato-born friend, Anita Andrade, an incredible cook who works with me at my restaurants. The secret weapon? Coca-Cola.

★ Preheat the oven to 450°F.

★ Blend the garlic, onion, oregano, thyme, salt, and ½ cup of water in a blender until fairly smooth.

★ Combine the pork and bay leaves in a 6-quart Dutch oven or deep baking dish that can hold the pork in no more than 2 layers. Pour the blended mixture and the Coca-Cola over the pork and stir and toss well.

★ Cover the pot and cook in the oven until the pork is very tender, about 2 hours. The sides of the pot might look dark. That's just fine.

★ Uncover the pot and return it to the oven. Continue cooking, tossing well and scraping the bottom of the pot every 10 minutes, until the pork is slightly crispy on the outside and deep golden brown, about 30 minutes. Coarsely shred the pork.

★ **MAKE AHEAD:** You can make carnitas up to three days before you plan to serve them.

★ Serve alongside **24 WARM CORN TORTILLAS** and **LIME WEDGES** and top with **CHOPPED WHITE ONION, CHOPPED CILANTRO,** and **FRESH GREEN SALSA** (page 133), **JALAPEÑO AND PINEAPPLE SALSA** (page 131), or **PICO DE GALLO WITH LEMON ZEST** (page 127).

TACOS of PORK with PINEAPPLE
Tacos al pastor

☆ ★ ★ ★ ★ A A A A A ☆ ☆ ☆ ☆ ☆ ☆

Nearly every Mexico City native has a soft spot for *tacos al pastor*, tortillas cradling marinated pork and little chunks of pineapple in which some taquerias specialize. Watching the meat rotate on a vertical spit, you can't help but be reminded of the gyro and shawarma of the Middle East, from which these tacos undoubtedly derive. (To drive that point home, in some Mexican precincts, you can order *tacos árabes*, a similar preparation of meat served on pita bread.) I've come up with an easy, if untraditional, way to re-create the flavors at home—no spit necessary.

★ Soak the guajillo chiles in enough water to cover until they're soft, about 30 minutes. Drain them and discard the water.

★ Meanwhile, preheat a small dry pan over medium-low heat. Roast the habanero chile in the pan until it's soft, blistered all over, and blackened in spots, 8 to 12 minutes. Cut the habanero in half and reserve one half for another purpose.

★ Blend the guajillos and habanero with the spice blend, garlic, ginger, vinegar, salt, and 2 tablespoons of fresh water until the mixture is very smooth, about 2 minutes.

★ Put the pork in a large bowl, add 6 tablespoons of the chile mixture, and use your hands (and gloves, if you have them) to rub the mixture all over each slice. Cover the bowl and marinate the pork in the fridge for at least 2 hours or overnight.

★ Cut the pork into large pieces, if necessary. Season lightly with salt.

★ Heat a grill or large heavy pan over high heat, add a slick of oil to the pan. When it begins to smoke, work in batches to avoid crowding the pan, and cook the pork until it is deep brown on both sides and cooked through, about 3 minutes, adding more oil as necessary. Cut into slices or small pieces.

★ Serve alongside **24 WARM CORN TORTILLAS** and **LIME WEDGES** and top with **CHOPPED WHITE ONION, CHOPPED CILANTRO, DICED PINEAPPLE,** and **FRESH GREEN SALSA** (page 133), with or without avocado.

FOR THE PORK:

6 dried guajillo chiles (about 1½ ounces), wiped clean, stemmed, split open, seeded, and deveined

1 fresh habanero chile

3 tablespoons Easy Annatto Spice Blend (page 50)

6 large garlic cloves, peeled

1 tablespoon chopped peeled ginger

½ cup distilled white vinegar

2 tablespoons kosher salt

2 pounds boneless pork chops, pounded to ⅛-inch thick

About 2 tablespoons olive or vegetable oil

→ **MAKES 24 TACOS ★**

YUCATÁN-STYLE PORK TACOS
Tacos de cochinita pibil

☆ ☆

FOR THE PORK:

5 tablespoons Easy Annatto Spice Blend (page 50)

5 tablespoons distilled white vinegar

¼ cup freshly squeezed orange juice

2 tablespoons freshly squeezed lime juice

5 large garlic cloves, peeled

2 tablespoons kosher salt

4 pounds boneless pork shoulder, with fat cap removed, cut into 2-inch chunks

3 or 4 large banana leaves, thawed if frozen, wiped clean on both sides (optional)

·····················
→ MAKES 20 TACOS ★
·····················

You may have sampled this tangle of meltingly tender pork, perhaps the most famous culinary export of the Yucatán, even if you've never visited Mérida. Before it's wrapped in banana leaves, the meat is rubbed with a paste made from citrus—traditionally sour orange, but for our purposes, a mixture of orange and lime juice—and achiote seeds. Also called annatto seeds, the red, pebble-like seeds of the annatto tree give the pork a very particular (and very lovable) flavor and a gorgeous orange hue. Whether you take the extra step to find banana leaves or just use aluminum foil, you'll be thrilled by the result, especially if you serve it with its nearly inseparable partner: bright pink pickled onions.

~~~~~~

★ Preheat the oven to 300°F.

★ Add the spice mixture with the vinegar, citrus juices, garlic, salt, and 5 tablespoons of water to a blender and blend until very smooth, at least a minute.

★ Put the pork in a deep baking dish or Dutch oven large enough to fit the pork in more or less one layer. (If using the banana leaves, line the dish with them before adding the pork and fold them over the top before covering with the lid.) Rub the blended mixture onto the pork to coat each piece well. Tightly cover the dish with foil or a tight-fitting lid and cook the pork in the oven until it is tender enough to cut with a spoon, about 2½ hours. If the pork looks very liquidy, remove the lid for the last 30 minutes of cooking.

★ **MAKE AHEAD:** Cooled and refrigerated, the pork keeps for up to three days.

★ Serve alongside **20 WARM CORN TORTILLAS, PICKLED RED ONIONS** (page 147) and **TOMATO-HABANERO SALSA** (page 128).

MARINATED SKIRT STEAK TACOS

Tacos de carne asada

☆ ☆ ☆ ☆ ☆ ☆ ☆ ☆ ☆ ☆ ☆ ☆ ☆ ☆ ☆ ☆ ☆ ★ ★ ★ ★ ★ ★ ★ ☆ ☆ ☆ ☆ ☆ ☆ ☆ ☆ ☆

I took all the flavors I love to pair with steak—mustard, lime juice, Worcestershire sauce, and more—and blended them to create this simple marinade. Skirt is my cut of choice, because it's full of flavor and has a tender texture with just a touch of lovely chew.

★ Combine all the ingredients, except the steak, in a blender jar, and blend until fairly smooth. You might have to pulse at first and prod the marinade with a spoon to help it blend.

★ Put the steak in a large bowl and pour in the marinade. Rub the marinade onto the steak with your fingers to make sure it's well coated all over. Cover the bowl with plastic wrap and refrigerate it for at least 1 hour or up to 3 hours.

★ Preheat a grill or heavy skillet over high heat. Cook the steak, in batches if necessary, turning it over once, until both sides are well browned and the steaks are cooked to your liking, about 4 minutes per side for medium rare. Let the steaks rest on a plate for about 3 minutes, then cut them against the grain into slices, then again into small pieces.

★ Serve alongside **12 WARM CORN TORTILLAS** spread with **PECAN-CHIPOTLE SALSA** (page 140). Or serve with tortillas and **LIME WEDGES** and top with **CHOPPED WHITE ONION, CHOPPED CILANTRO,** and **JALAPEÑO AND PINEAPPLE SALSA** (page 137) or **FRIED CHILE SALSA** (page 138).

FOR THE STEAK:

⅓ cup coarsely chopped cilantro

½ small red onion, roughly chopped

½ medium fresh serrano or jalapeño chile (including seeds)

1 medium garlic clove, peeled

1 tablespoon freshly squeezed lime juice

1 tablespoon olive or vegetable oil

1 tablespoon Worcestershire sauce

2 teaspoons kosher salt

1 teaspoon Dijon mustard

¼ teaspoon freshly ground black pepper

2 pounds trimmed skirt steak, cut widthwise into 3 or 4 pieces

→ **MAKES 12 TACOS** ★

TONGUE TACOS
Tacos de lengua

☆ ☆

FOR THE TONGUE:

1 (4-pound) beef tongue (thawed, if frozen), rinsed well under running water

1 pound white onions (about 2 medium), peeled and quartered

10 medium garlic cloves, peeled

2 tablespoons kosher salt

3 dried bay leaves

3 whole cloves

2 teaspoons dried Mexican oregano

1 teaspoon dried thyme

About 2 tablespoons olive or vegetable oil

→ **MAKES 12 TO 16 TACOS ★**

Beloved in Mexico, a country also in love with ears, snouts, and feet, tongue is often avoided in the U.S. Yet I urge you to try it slowly simmered then crisped on a griddle, because its impossibly tender texture and big beefy flavor have converted many a reluctant taco-eater. The tongue is just as good simmered a day or two before you plan to serve it.

★ Put the tongue in a deep pot; feel free to bend it if you need to. Add the remaining ingredients, except for the oil, and enough cold water to cover the tongue by an inch or two. Cover the pot and bring the water to a boil over high heat, then lower the heat to maintain a steady simmer. Cook, carefully turning over the tongue with tongs every hour and adding more hot water if the water level falls below two-thirds of the way up the tongue, until the tongue is very tender but not falling apart, about 3¼ hours. You should be able to insert a sharp knife or skewer into the thick rear and thinner tip of the tongue and get almost no resistance in either place.

★ Let the tongue sit in the cooking liquid until it's just cool enough to handle. Peel off the tough skin and bumpy layer underneath the skin (although many cooks in Mexico leave this be). Trim off the fatty, sinewy part underneath the tongue and towards the back of the tongue but reserve any meaty parts. Return the peeled, trimmed tongue to the liquid, let it cool completely.

★ MAKE AHEAD: Wrap and keep it in the fridge overnight or for up to 2 days.

★ Drain the liquid from the tongue, then cut the tongue into small pieces. Heat a large pan over medium-high heat. Add just enough oil to form a thin sheen in the pan. When the oil is lightly smoking, add the tongue pieces in batches, season generously with salt, if necessary, and cook until lightly brown, 3 to 4 minutes.

★ Serve alongside **12 TO 16 WARM CORN TORTILLAS** and **LIME WEDGES** and top with **CHOPPED WHITE ONION**, **CHOPPED CILANTRO**, and **JALAPEÑO AND PINEAPPLE SALSA** (page 137) or **FRESH GUAJE SALSA** (page 142).

EASY ANNATTO SPICE BLEND
Recado rojo

Sure, you could use jarred achiote paste to make my Yucatán-style pork (page 44) and pork al pastor (page 43), but you'll be sure to reach taco heaven if you make it yourself from whole spices. Once upon a time, before electric grinders were so accessible, making this simple spice mixture took hours and hours of soaking and laboriously grinding on the flat stone mortar called a *metate*. Today, it takes all of a minute.

6 tablespoons annatto (achiote) seeds

3 tablespoons dried Mexican oregano

3 whole cloves

2 scant teaspoons cumin seeds

1 teaspoon whole allspice berries

1 scant teaspoon whole black peppercorns

★ Grind the spices in a spice grinder or clean coffee grinder to a fine powder.

★ MAKE AHEAD: The spice mixture keeps in an airtight container stored in a dry, dark place for several months.

→ **MAKES ABOUT 10 TABLESPOONS**

FRYING FLOUR
Harina para freír

A great all-purpose mixture for whatever you're frying, be it chicken cutlets for tortas (page 74) or fish for salpicón (page 31).

1 cup all-purpose flour

4 teaspoons árbol chile powder or chipotle powder (see page 210)

1 tablespoon dried Mexican oregano, crumbled

½ teaspoon ground cumin

1 tablespoon kosher salt

★ Combine the flour, chile powder, oregano, cumin, and salt in a large bowl, and mix very well.

★ MAKE AHEAD: The flour keeps in an airtight container stored in a dry, dark place for a few weeks.

→ **MAKES A GENEROUS CUP**

CHOPPED LIVER TACOS
Tacos de higaditos

☆ ★ ▲ ▲ ▲ ☆

I get giddy when I spot chicken liver lurking in the *cazuelas* at the small shops and market stalls that sell *tacos de guisado*. The mild, slightly creamy liver is such a pleasure, especially paired with the sweetness of onions and brightness of lime. When I was a boy, I'd swear I never had the thought, though now that I'm a New Yorker with plenty of Jewish friends, I can't help but think of chopped liver when I make these today.

★ Heat 1 tablespoon of the oil in a large pan over medium-high heat until it shimmers. Add the onions, chiles, and ¼ teaspoon of the salt and cook, stirring frequently, until the onions are very soft and browned at the edges, about 8 minutes. Transfer the mixture to a large bowl.

★ Generously season the livers on both sides with salt (about ½ teaspoon) and pepper, if you'd like. Heat the remaining 2 tablespoons of oil in the same large pan over high heat. Working in batches to avoid crowding the pan, cook the livers until they're nicely browned on both sides and just barely pink in the center, 3 to 4 minutes per batch. Transfer them to the bowl with the onions as they're done.

★ Add the contents of the bowl back to the hot pan and cook, stirring frequently and mashing a little, for a minute or two. Add the lime juice and season to taste with salt.

★ Serve alongside **12 WARM CORN TORTILLAS** and top with **CHOPPED CILANTRO** and **TOMATILLO-ÁRBOL SALSA** (page 134) or **AVOCADO-TOMATILLO SALSA** (page 133).

FOR THE LIVER:

3 tablespoons olive or vegetable oil

1 pound white onions, thinly sliced into half-moons

2 fresh serrano or jalapeño chiles, thinly sliced lengthwise (including seeds)

¾ teaspoon kosher salt

1 pound chicken livers, cut into lobes and trimmed of any tough white parts

Freshly ground black pepper

2 tablespoons freshly squeezed lime juice

→ **MAKES 12 TACOS** ★

GROUND BEEF, OLIVE, AND RAISIN TACOS
Tacos de picadillo

Remember when every taco in America seemed to be filled with ground beef? The source was likely picadillo, but places like Taco Bell totally missed the boat, turning a truly delicious dish into an inscrutable meat mush. Derived from the Spanish verb *picar*, meaning "to chop," picadillo refers to a mixture of chopped ingredients that has as many variations as it does people who cook it. In addition to or in place of the components listed here, you might find potatoes or zucchini or fried ripe plantains. Whatever you choose to use, each bite will be different, some bringing the salty punch of olives and capers and others providing a hit of sweetness from raisins or the crunch of almonds. Besides making great tacos, picadillo is great as the filling for tortas, enchiladas, and chiles rellenos, or just a fine topper for rice.

★ Heat the oil in a medium pot over medium-high heat. Add the onions and a generous pinch of salt, and cook, stirring occasionally, until the onions are translucent, about 5 minutes. Add the garlic, cook for a minute, then add the tomatoes, bay leaves, thyme, sugar, vinegar, and 1 teaspoon of the salt. Let the mixture come to a boil, then lower the heat to maintain a vigorous simmer, and cook, stirring occasionally, until almost all the liquid has evaporated, about 45 minutes. Transfer the mixture to a bowl.

(Continued on page 54.)

FOR THE PICADILLO:

3 tablespoons olive or vegetable oil

2 cups diced white onions

2 teaspoons kosher salt

3 large garlic cloves, finely chopped

2¼ pounds ripe tomatoes, cored and chopped

2 dried bay leaves

½ teaspoon dried thyme

1 teaspoon sugar

2 teaspoons apple cider vinegar

1 pound lean ground beef

1 pound lean ground pork

Freshly ground black pepper

Generous ½ cup pimento-stuffed manzanilla olives, halved (or sliced, if large)

¼ cup raisins

3 tablespoons finely chopped pickled jalapeño chiles, including a little of their liquid

1 tablespoon drained capers

¼ cup slivered almonds

¼ cup chopped cilantro

Generous 2 tablespoons chopped flat-leaf parsley

Generous 2 tablespoons chopped fresh spearmint leaves

→ **MAKES 24 TACOS** ★

★ Wipe out the pot, set it over high heat, and when it's hot, add the ground beef and pork without any oil. Season with freshly ground black pepper and ¾ teaspoon kosher salt. Cook, stirring and breaking up the meat, until it is cooked through, then add the olives, raisins, pickled jalapeños, and capers. Cook until the liquid from the meat has evaporated, about 5 minutes. Add the tomato mixture and lower the heat to medium. Cover and cook until the flavors have melded, about 5 minutes, then stir in the almonds and herbs.

★ Serve alongside **24 WARM CORN TORTILLAS** and top with **SLICED CANNED PICKLED JALAPEÑO CHILES, CRUMBLED QUESO FRESCO**, and slices of **RIPE MEXICAN HASS AVOCADO**.

SLOW-COOKED LAMB TACOS
Tacos de barbacoa de borrego

☆ ☆

Pit-cooked, spice-rubbed lamb is such an iconic dish that it inspires entire taquerias devoted to its exultation.

★ Preheat the oven to 350°F.

★ Preheat a large pan over medium-low heat. Toast the ancho, guajillo, and árbol chiles, turning them over and pressing down on them with tongs frequently, until the anchos and guajillos are fragrant, about 1 to 1½ minutes, and the árbol chiles have browned all over with some dark spots, 3 to 4 minutes. Soak the chiles in enough cold water to cover until they're soft, about 20 minutes. Drain, discarding the water.

★ Blend the chiles with the vinegar, the garlic, cumin, oregano, cloves, salt, and ½ cup of fresh water in a blender to form a very smooth puree, at least 3 minutes.

★ Put the lamb in a deep baking dish or a Dutch oven just large enough to hold it, then rub the adobo all over the meat and pour any remaining adobo over it. Swish ¼ cup water in the blender and add it to the pot. Cover the pot with a tight-fitting lid or two layers of heavy-duty foil. Cook in the oven, basting occasionally, until the meat is fork-tender, about 2½ hours.

★ Coarsely shred the meat with tongs and return it to the sauce in the Dutch oven. Season to taste with more vinegar and salt.

★ MAKE AHEAD: The saucy shredded lamb keeps in the fridge for up to three days or in the freezer for up to one month.

★ Serve alongside 16 TO 20 WARM CORN TORTILLAS and LIME WEDGES and top with CHOPPED WHITE ONION, CHOPPED CILANTRO, and FRIED CHILE SALSA (page 138) or PICO DE GALLO WITH LEMON ZEST (page 127).

FOR THE LAMB:

2 dried ancho chiles (about 1 ounce), wiped clean, stemmed, seeded, and deveined

2 dried guajillo chiles (about ½ ounce), wiped clean, stemmed, slit open, seeded, and deveined

4 dried árbol chiles (about 1 ounce), wiped clean and stemmed (optional)

2 tablespoons apple cider vinegar, or more to taste

5 large garlic cloves, peeled

1 teaspoon cumin seeds

1 teaspoon dried Mexican oregano

4 whole cloves

2 teaspoons kosher salt

1 (2½-pound) boneless lamb shoulder roast

→ MAKES 16 TO 20 TACOS ★

★ ★ ★

TORTAS

☆ ☆

FOR A SECOND, YOU THINK you're in Paris. Bakeries on every corner are selling crusty bread, butter cookies, and *palmiers*, the pastries shaped like elephant ears you might get in Montmarte. You almost expect to hear a worker ask, "*Je vous en prie*?" That is, until you see sweets topped with Froot Loops cereal. You're not in France—you're in Mexico, where baked goods are about as common as tortillas.

I love Mexican breads like *teleras* and *bolillos* most of all, perhaps because it's these breads that become "tortas." Forced to translate into English, we all go with "sandwich," though that's a bit like describing a Rembrandt masterpiece as a portrait—it's accurate but it doesn't do justice to the work of art.

If you visit Mexico, you'll see tortas everywhere—at streetside stalls, at markets, in devoted restaurants (called *torterías*), and in people's homes. Virtually anything tasty can wind up in a torta—the luscious *carnitas* made in giant vats in Michoacán? But of course. Scrambled eggs? Why not? A flavor-packed jumble of chorizo and potatoes? Absolutely! In Mexico City, you'll even see construction workers biting into tortas made from canned sardines and pickled jalapeños.

Like virtually all foods in Mexico, local variations abound. In the state of Guanajuato, sandwich masters pile *bolillos* with crunchy fried pork skins, hard-boiled eggs, and crispy *tacos de nada*—bean-filled tortillas fried until the beans seem to disappear, hence their English translation: "tacos of nothing." Anyone visiting Guadalajara must try the city's specialty: *torta ahogada*, or "drowned torta," which gets doused in salsa. Just as some American sandwiches are so distinctive that they deserve names all their own—I'm thinking of the Philly cheesesteak, Buffalo's beef on weck, and New Orleans's po'boys, among others—many Mexican sandwiches do too. That strange but wonderful sandwich from Guanajuato is called a *guacamaya*. The *cemita*, the iconic sandwich of Puebla, is served on an eponymous sesame-seed roll and typically stacked high with meat, cheese, pickled chipotles, and an unforgettably distinctive herb called *papalo*. For the *pambazos* of Mexico City, vendors construct the sandwich, dunk it in mild chile sauce, then fry the whole thing.

While certain classic combinations endure, there are no rules to torta construction. Put it on a roll, and you've got the beginnings of a torta. Because mere deliciousness is never enough for us Mexicans, we pile on more layers of texture and flavor. That means salty, squeaky cheese; creamy avocado slices; and refried beans along with standards like lettuce and tomato. Many tortas include a little something to set your mouth ablaze, everything from chipotles in adobo (straight from the can), pickled jalapeño chiles (ditto!), or cool, crunchy pico de gallo.

Many of my favorite tortas take barely any effort at all. Sometimes I lay a few slices of cheese between two slices of ham, then into the skillet they go until the ham is a little crispy and cheese is molten. A good roll, a few pickled jalapeños, a tremendously tasty sandwich.

☆ ☆

PORTABLE PLEASURE

There are many reasons a taco-loving people might readily adopt the torta. My theory: The torta took all the foods people already loved and made them portable. Once it's encased in bread, all that flavor can travel wherever you go: the park, the plane, the office. (My friends and I joke that government bureaucrats always seem to wipe off their fingers right before they handle your paperwork, because they have a torta hiding in the drawer.) And it's not just typical torta fillings that end up stuffed inside a roll. You'll even see stand-alone dishes, like saucy moles and wonderfully greasy tamales or the sauce-doused tortilla chips called *chilaquiles*. These carb-on-carb combinations seem crazy even to many Mexicans, but just try eating a plate of *chilaquiles* while you're dodging the rush-hour crowd on the way to work, and you'll understand why these funky tortas are so popular.

ON A ROLL

Order a torta in other Spanish-speaking countries and you'll get a cake. Only in Mexico does the word mean "sandwich." The word *sandwich* exists in Mexican Spanish, too, but it immediately conjures meat or cheese between sliced bread. Say the word "torta" to a Mexican, and he'll know right away that you're referring to a sandwich on a roll. Sometimes this roll is a crusty *bolillo*, but more often it's a *telera*, which is barely crusty on the outside and soft and fluffy inside, with two indentations running along the top. With a few exceptions, the torta recipes in this book call for *teleras*. Almost every Mexican bakery sells *teleras* and *bolillos*, but if you

don't live near a good one, don't worry—I've come up with some excellent substitutes and even provided a recipe for making your own. As you make your tortas, keep in mind that roll sizes vary, so use your judgment when you assemble them. If you're short on filling, just load up on the toppings!

THE BEST SUSTITUTE: Portuguese rolls, with their unobtrusive flavor and airy crumb, make a great stand-in for *teleras*. In fact, I prefer a good Portuguese roll to a mediocre *telera*.

THE NEXT BEST THING: If you can't find Portuguese rolls, look for kaiser rolls, ciabatta (either individual rolls or a larger loaf cut into pieces), or even a good French baguette.

A FEW EXCEPTIONS: *Guacamayas* and *tortas ahogados* call for *bolillos* (technically, the latter are made with a roll called a *birote*, which is like Guadalajara's version of a *bolillo*). Although baguettes have a different shape, I find they make an excellent *bolillo* stand-in.

➡ **HEAVEN IN A CAN:** *Pickled jalapeños lend their indispensable flavor to so many tortas, providing a spicy, tart break from all those rich toppings like meat, avocado, cheese, and cream. Fortunately for all of us, the canned kind found at supermarkets around the country is quite delicious, an essential part of my pantry. When you add them to your sandwich, don't neglect the liquid they come in: I like to add my slices still dripping so I can be sure the sandwich receives the jolt of acidity I'm looking for.*

BETTER BREAD

With almost any rolls, from brioche to kaiser, I find it helps to split them and pinch off and discard some of the soft crumb before toasting them. This ensures a more friendly bread-to-filling ratio and, to me, a tastier torta.

RESURRECTING LIFELESS BREAD

It's not always easy to find great rolls. Yet if the only rolls you can get are overly doughy or squishy and textureless, you're not out of luck. You'll be amazed at how lifeless bread becomes crispy-crusted and inviting after this trick: Preheat the oven to 450°F. Splash a bit of water on your hands, rub it onto the whole rolls, then stick the rolls in the oven until they're warm to the core and have come back to life, 3 to 5 minutes.

COLD TORTAS

Every Monday when I was a kid, my family had lunch at my grandma's house. Sometimes she'd cook elaborate, multi-course meals. But when she was in a rush, she'd serve tortas. On her table she'd set out a massive spread: fresh *teleras* from her favorite bakery, ham and head cheese, queso fresco and queso Oaxaca, and avocado slices, not to mention a host of condiments from mustard to crema. Cold tortas make a fine option for a picnic, so long as you wrap them in wax paper, not plastic, so they can breathe a little.

HOT TORTAS

I remember being mesmerized when my parents took me to get hot tortas, less common on the streets than they are in dedicated *torterías*. I'd sit on a stool, barely able to see over the counter, and watch the cooks working at top speed—chopping and frying and stacking, shuffling what seemed like a thousand rolls on the hot flat-top grill. There are generally two types of hot tortas: those made with griddled fillings (*tortas calientes* or *a la plancha*), such as tender shredded roasted pork leg or ham, and those made with stewed fillings (*tortas de guisado*), such as moles, tomato-spiked salt cod, and even octopus!

These tortas are not constructed then griddled, like panini. Instead, the bread is heated in a pan first. That's the magic part. Once you learn the basic blueprint, you'll find yourself tempted never to make another type of sandwich again.

- Preheat a griddle or pan over medium heat. Spread butter (this is optional but recommended) on both sides of the split roll and cook the rolls, cut sides down, until they are light golden brown and crisp, but still soft in the middle, 30 seconds to a minute.
- Heat the filling in a pan.
- Spread refried beans on the bottom half of the roll and the Mexican crema or mayonnaise and/or mustard on the top half.
- Add the filling to the bottom half and top with avocado, cheese, pickled jalapeños, or whatever else you'd like.

TELERAS

☆ ☆

1½ cups warm water (100° to 110°F)

2¼ teaspoons active dry yeast (one ¼ ounce envelope)

1 cup whole milk, at room temperature

6¾ cups (1¾ pounds) unbleached bread flour, plus extra for dusting

2 tablespoons plus 2 teaspoons kosher salt

1 tablespoon sugar

Non stick cooking spray

EQUIPMENT:

Stand mixer with a dough hook attachment

Parchment paper

→ **MAKES 10 TELERAS** ★

A huge thanks to my dear friend, the baking guru Nick Malgieri, for helping me develop this recipe for teleras. Believe me, you *can* do this at home. When you do, imagine Nick looking over your shoulder, as he did over mine, gently scolding me when I was tempted to use a liquid cup measure for flour (you must use a dry measure!) and when I tried to scoop flour straight from the bag (it's much better to pour flour into a bowl and fluff it, then measure it, using a knife to level off each cup). This is baking, after all. Precision counts!

MAKE THE DOUGH:

★ In the bowl of a stand mixer fitted with a dough hook, add the warm water and whisk in the yeast. Whisk in the milk.

★ In a separate bowl, mix the flour, salt, and sugar together well. Use a flexible spatula or a wooden spoon to stir the dry ingredients into the yeast mixture until it's well mixed. Starting at the lowest speed, mix the dough for 2 minutes, then increase the speed one notch and mix for another 2 minutes. Increase the speed another notch and mix for another 2 minutes or until you have a nice, elastic dough wrapped around the dough hook. Spray a large bowl with non-stick spray and transfer the dough to the bowl.

★ Cover the bowl with a kitchen towel and leave it at room temperature until the dough doubles in volume, about 1 hour or more, depending on the temperature and humidity in the room. (For an even better flavor and texture, use your fist to press firmly against the risen dough several times, then cover and refrigerate it overnight before moving on to the next step.)

FORM AND COOK THE TELERAS:

★ Gather the dough into a long rectangular shape on a lightly-floured work surface. Cut the sticky, wobbly dough into 10 equal-sized pieces. Dust a large kitchen towel with flour. Use your palm to "round" each piece of dough: cup your palm and apply light pressure to roll the dough into a ball. Invert the round (smooth, rounded side down) onto the floured towel. Cover the dough rounds with another towel and let them rest for 10 minutes.

★ Working with one at a time, turn the dough rounds smooth sides up on a floured work surface, dust them with flour, and press lightly with your palm to flatten slightly. Pull the sides of each piece of round dough to form an oval shape and dust again with flour.

★ Use the handle of a wooden spoon (or a ½-inch thick dowel) to press on each oval to make two parallel, lengthwise indentations that appear to divide each oval into thirds. Press firmly so that the handle almost touches the work surface. Put them, indented sides up, on two large baking sheets lined with parchment paper. Cover again and let the rolls double in size, about an hour.

★ Preheat the oven to 425°F. Bake, turning the trays after 10 minutes, just until the rolls have turned light golden brown and when you tap on them with a finger, they sound hollow, about 15 to 18 minutes.

★ Let the rolls cool, uncovered. Use them right away, store them in a bag at room temperature for up to a day, or freeze any extra teleras in airtight freezer bags for up to one month.

The Sardine Torta

☆ ☆ ☆

A funky classic eaten by construction workers, this sandwich will satisfy anyone in need of a quick, tasty lunch.

☆ ☆ ☆

Drain a small can of sardines, invert it onto a roll, and top with queso fresco, avocado slices, pickled jalapeños, and a spoonful or two of Pico de Gallo (page 127).

MOLLETES

☆ ☆

This is the Mexican equivalent to the American grilled-cheese or turkey sandwich, an everyday treat you throw together with what's in the fridge. In Mexico, that's beans, cheese, and salsa. Though *molletes* are available in restaurants, they're definitely best made at home, when you can make sure to properly butter and toast the bread, add the right amount of beans and cheese, then melt that queso under the broiler.

★ Preheat the oven or toaster oven to 500°F.

★ Heat a large pan over medium heat until it's nice and hot. Spread the butter over the cut sides of the roll halves. Place them, cut sides down, in the pan and cook until they are lightly golden brown and crispy, a minute or two.

★ Spread a thin layer of beans over the toasted side of each roll. Top with a thin layer of cheese. Cook the *molletes* (open-faced) in the oven just until the cheese has melted and turned golden brown in a few spots, 3 to 5 minutes.

★ Serve the *molletes* beside a bowl of the pico de gallo.

1 tablespoon unsalted butter, softened

2 large rolls, preferably teleras, Portuguese, kaiser, or ciabatta, split

Generous ¼ cup Refried Black Beans, homemade (page 148) or canned

6 ounces Chihuahua or provolone cheese, shredded

Generous ½ cup Pico de Gallo with Lemon Zest (page 127)

→ **MAKES 4** ★

BOLOGNA TORTA
Torta de mortadela

☆ ☆

8 (¼-inch-thick) slices
    bologna or mortadella
    (about ¾ pound)

⅔ pound provolone cheese,
    cut into ¼-inch-thick slices

About 1 teaspoon olive or
    vegetable oil

About 3 tablespoons
    unsalted butter, softened

4 large rolls, preferably
    teleras, Portuguese, kaiser,
    or ciabatta, split

½ cup Refried Pinto Beans,
    homemade (page 148) or
    canned

3 tablespoons mayonnaise

4 teaspoons Dijon or yellow
    mustard

. . . .
→ MAKES 4 ★
. . . .

When I was growing up, there was a cartoon character called Mortadelo, named for Italian mortadella or what Americans call bologna. I adore bologna and I know no better way to eat it than in torta form, thanks to the spark of pickled jalapeños and the melty cheese sandwiched by crispy bologna slices.

★ Top 4 bologna slices with the cheese slices, dividing equally. Top each stack with another slice of bologna.

★ Heat a large nonstick skillet over medium-high heat. Add the oil to the hot pan, and when it shimmers, add the bologna-cheese stacks (work in batches to avoid crowding the pan). Cook until the bologna is golden brown and the cheese inside has melted, about 1 minute per side.

★ Spread the butter evenly over the cut sides of the rolls. Cook the rolls, buttered sides down, in the skillet until they are light golden brown and crisp, but still soft in the middle, a minute or two.

★ Spread a layer of beans (a tablespoon or two) over the bottom half of each roll and spread the mayonnaise and mustard over the roll tops. Add the bologna stacks to the roll bottoms. Top with **THINLY SLICED WHITE ONION**, slices of **RIPE MEXICAN HASS AVOCADO**, a pinch of salt, and **SLICED CANNED PICKLED JALAPEÑOS, CANNED CHIPOTLES IN ADOBO**, or **PICKLED CHIPOTLES** (page 146). Cover with the roll tops and press firmly but gently.

→ **HAM AND CHEESE TORTAS** (*Tortas de jamón y queso*)
One of my favorite weeknight tortas, and virtually identical to the torta de mortadela. *You just swap sliced ham for bologna.*

GRILLED HOT DOG TORTAS
Tortas de salchicha

☆ ☆

Virtually every *tortería* serves this torta, split hot dogs griddled and tucked inside bread. Instead of ketchup and relish, you dress your dog with all the typical torta condiments. Good old yellow American cheese provides another melty flavor and texture. It's not diet food, that's for sure, but it sure is delicious.

About 3 tablespoons un-salted butter, softened

4 large rolls, preferably teleras, Portuguese, kaiser, or ciabatta, split

½ cup Refried Black Beans, homemade (page 148) or canned

8 thin slices yellow American cheese

Scant ¼ cup Mexican crema or crème fraîche

4 teaspoons Dijon or yellow mustard

6 fully-cooked beef hot dogs (2 ounces each), halved lengthwise

★ Heat a large nonstick skillet over medium-high heat. Spread the butter evenly over the cut sides of the rolls. Cook the rolls, buttered sides down, in the skillet until they are light golden brown and crisp, but still soft in the middle, a minute or two.

★ Spread a layer of beans (a tablespoon or two) over the bottom half of each roll, then put a slice of cheese on the roll bottoms. Spread the crema and mustard over the roll tops and add the remaining cheese.

★ Cook the hot dogs, cut side down, in the same pan until they're golden brown, about 2 minutes per side. Set the bun bottoms, cheese side down, on top of the hot dogs. Cook for a minute more, so the cheese has a chance to melt.

★ Flip the bun bottoms and the hot dogs together onto a cutting board. Top with SLICED CANNED PICKLED JALAPEÑOS, THINLY SLICED WHITE ONIONS, slices of RIPE MEXICAN HASS AVOCADO, and a pinch of salt. Cover with the roll tops and press firmly but gently.

→ **MAKES 4** ★

STEWED FRANKFURTER TORTAS

Tortas de salchichas guisadas

☆ ☆

1 tablespoon olive or vegetable oil

1 pound all-beef hot dogs (about 8), cut crosswise into ¼-inch slices

1 small white onion, thinly sliced into half-moons

2 large fresh serrano or jalapeño chiles, thinly sliced lengthwise into strips (including seeds)

2 medium garlic cloves, finely chopped

2 dried bay leaves

½ pound tomato (about 1 large), finely chopped

1 canned chipotle chile in adobo, finely chopped (optional)

Kosher salt

About 3 tablespoons unsalted butter, softened

4 large rolls, preferably teleras, Portuguese, kaiser, or ciabatta, split

½ cup Refried Black Beans, homemade (page 148) or canned

3 tablespoons mayonnaise

. . . .
→ **MAKES 4** ★
. . . .

The Mexican love for sausage on display once more, stewed hot dogs are a common taco and torta filling. My American friends always smirk when I serve them this, but after their first bite, they're all smiles. I like to add a layer of beans to the bottom rolls, not just because it's delicious but also because it helps keep the roll from getting soggy.

★ Heat the oil in a large pan over medium-high heat until it shimmers. Add the hot dogs, onion, jalapeños, garlic, and bay leaves, and cook, stirring occasionally, until the onion is translucent and the hot dogs are lightly browned, about 8 minutes.

★ Add the tomatoes and the chipotle, if you're using it. Let them come to a simmer, and cook until some of the liquid from the tomatoes has evaporated but the mixture still looks moist, about 8 minutes. Season to taste with salt.

★ Heat a large nonstick skillet over medium-high heat. Spread the butter evenly over the cut sides of the rolls. Cook the rolls, buttered sides down, in the skillet until they are light golden brown and crisp, but still soft in the middle, a minute or two.

★ Spread a layer of beans (a tablespoon or two) over the bottom half of each roll and spread the mayonnaise over the roll tops. Top the roll bottoms with the stew and slices of **RIPE MEXICAN HASS AVOCADO**, then cover with the roll tops and press firmly but gently.

→ **NOTE ON BEEF:** *If you're using tenderloin, cut the meat into thin, round slices and use several per sandwich. If you're using strip or rib-eye, have your butcher slice the steaks horizontally and use one per sandwich.*

→ **EVEN MORE FLAVOR:** *The beef for pepitos needs nothing more than a sprinkle of salt and pepper. But if you'd like even more flavor, try coating it in the marinade for skirt steak tacos (page 47) before you cook it.*

STEAK SANDWICH
Pepito

☆☆☆☆☆☆☆☆☆☆☆☆☆☆☆☆☆☆☆☆☆☆☆☆☆☆☆☆☆☆☆☆☆☆☆

This is a very Mexico City sandwich, an urban torta whose star is grilled sliced beef tenderloin. It's so common nowadays that you'll find it on the menu at VIPs, a popular chain restaurant, and San-born's, the department stores-slash-restaurants that seem to out-number Starbucks in Mexico City. As a seasoned pepito eater, I have a strict idea of its necessary condiments: refried black beans, sliced white onions, mayonnaise or crema, and maybe a little mustard. A little heat is essential, too—either pickled jalapeños, pico de gallo, or chipotle salsa. Take your pick.

★ Heat a large skillet or grill pan over high heat. Lay the beef on a large plate, and season it generously with salt and pepper on both sides. Pour the Worcestershire sauce and squeeze the lime over both sides of the beef.

★ Add enough oil to coat the bottom of the skillet in a very thin layer. Working in batches to avoid crowding the skillet, cook the beef until browned on both sides, 30 to 45 seconds per side. Transfer the beef to a clean plate to rest.

★ Reduce the heat to medium-low. Spread the butter evenly over the cut sides of the baguette. Cook the baguette pieces, buttered sides down, in the skillet until they are light golden brown and crisp, but still soft in the middle, a minute or two.

★ Spread a layer of beans (a tablespoon or two) over the baguette bottoms. Spread the mayonnaise and mustard over the baguette tops. Place the beef slices on the baguette bottoms, cutting and stacking the beef if necessary so it fits neatly on the baguette. Top with **SLICED CANNED PICKLED JALAPEÑOS** or **PICO DE GALLO WITH LEMON ZEST** (page 127), **THINLY SLICED WHITE ONION**, slices of **RIPE MEXICAN HASS AVOCADO**, and a pinch of salt. Cover with the baguette tops and press firmly but gently.

1 pound boneless beef tenderloin, or strip or rib eye steaks, sliced into ¼-inch-thick slices (see note)

Kosher salt and freshly ground black pepper

1 generous teaspoon Worcestershire sauce

½ juicy lime

Olive or vegetable oil

3 tablespoons unsalted butter, softened

1 baguette, cut into 4 equal pieces and split

½ cup Refried Black Beans, homemade (page 148) or canned

3 tablespoons mayonnaise or crema

4 teaspoons Dijon or yellow mustard

→ **MAKES 4** ★

CHICKEN CUTLET TORTAS
Tortas de milanesa de pollo

☆ ☆

¾ pound thin chicken breast cutlets, cut into 4 pieces

¾ teaspoon kosher salt

Freshly ground black pepper

1 large egg, beaten with 2 teaspoons water

½ recipe Frying Flour (page 50)

1½ cups panko bread crumbs

Canola or vegetable oil for shallow frying

About 3 tablespoons unsalted butter, softened

4 large rolls, preferably teleras, Portuguese, kaiser, or ciabatta, split

½ cup Refried Pinto Beans or Refried Black Beans, homemade (page 148) or canned

About ¼ cup Mexican crema, or 3 tablespoons mayonnaise

4 teaspoons Dijon or yellow mustard

→ **MAKES 4** ★

A crispy, juicy breaded cutlet in your torta—what's not to love? In Mexico, you're more likely to find cutlets made of pork and beef, sometimes pounded so thin they look like they're designed only to hold breadcrumbs. In the U.S., it's easier to find chicken cutlets, and breading and frying is a great way to add flavor and texture to the otherwise dull boneless, skinless chicken breast. But by all means, any Texans out there, feel free to substitute your favorite recipe for chicken-fried steak!

★ Season the chicken on both sides with the salt and pepper. Put the egg mixture, frying flour, and breadcrumbs in three separate shallow bowls. One by one, dip the chicken first in the egg mixture, tossing and rubbing to make sure it's very well coated; then in the flour mixture, patting and tossing to make sure it's well coated; then in the egg mixture again; and finally in the bread crumbs, patting and tossing until it's evenly coated. Transfer the breaded chicken to a plate as you finish.

★ Heat an inch of oil in a medium skillet over medium-high heat until it shimmers. (If you have a deep fat thermometer, heat the oil to 350 to 375°F.) Cook the cutlets, one at a time, turning them over once, until they're golden brown and crispy on both sides, about 3 minutes per side. Drain on paper towels.

★ Heat a large nonstick skillet over medium-high heat. Spread the butter evenly over the cut sides of the rolls. Cook the rolls, buttered sides down, in the skillet until they are light golden brown and crisp, but still soft in the middle, a minute or two.

★ Spread a layer of beans (a tablespoon or two) over the bottom half of each roll and spread the crema and mustard over the roll tops. Add the cutlets to the roll bottoms. Top with SLICED CANNED PICKLED JALAPEÑOS, THINLY SLICED WHITE ONION, slices of RIPE MEXICAN HASS AVOCADO, and a pinch of salt. Cover with the roll tops and press firmly but gently.

GUANAJUATO-STYLE CARNITAS TORTA
Torta de carnitas estilo Guanajuato

☆ ☆

4 cups carnitas (page 40)

About 3 tablespoons unsalted butter, softened

4 large rolls, preferably teleras, Portuguese, kaiser, or ciabatta, split

About ½ cup Creamy Avocado Sauce (page 149)

About 1 cup Guanajuato-Style Pico de Gallo (page 128)

....

→ **MAKES 4** ★

....

As soon as I get to Guanajuato, a pork-loving state in Central Mexico, I head straight to the market for the local take on the carnitas torta. The gorgeous chunks of pork come decked out with just two condiments: one a sauce made with avocado, chile—and often, mayonnaise—and a special pico de gallo. But that's all it takes to produce one of the greatest sandwiches you could imagine.

★ Heat a large nonstick skillet over medium-high heat.

★ Add the carnitas and cook until the meat is heated through and slightly crisp at the edges, about 5 minutes. Transfer to a plate or bowl. Spread the butter evenly over the cut sides of the rolls. Cook the rolls, buttered sides down, in the same skillet until they are light golden brown and crisp, but still soft in the middle, a minute or two.

★ Spoon about 1 cup of the carnitas onto each of the roll bottoms. Slather about 2 tablespoons of the avocado sauce on each roll top, then spoon about ¼ cup of the pico de gallo over the carnitas. Cover with the roll tops and press firmly but gently.

GUACAMAYA

☆☆☆☆☆☆☆☆☆☆☆☆☆☆☆☆☆☆☆☆☆☆☆☆☆☆☆☆☆☆☆☆☆

You can easily reproduce the pleasure of this unusual sandwich, local to the city of León in Guanajuato, at home.

★ Pile the chicharrones, eggs, and avocado slices on the rolls. Press down firmly to break up the chicharrones and egg slightly. Spoon on a generous amount of the pico de gallo, about ¼ cup per sandwich, then squeeze on some lime juice to taste, and serve.

¼ pound chicharrones (crunchy fried pork skins), broken into pieces

4 hard-boiled eggs, sliced

I large, ripe Mexican Hass avocado, peeled, pitted, and sliced at the last minute

4 large rolls, preferably bolillos, split, and some soft crust removed

About I cup Guanajuato-Style Pico de Gallo (page 128)

2 juicy limes

→ MAKES 4 ★

SALT COD TORTAS
Tortas de bacalao

¾ cup olive or vegetable oil

1 medium onion, thinly sliced into half-moons

¼ teaspoon kosher salt

4 large garlic cloves, finely chopped

3 large dried bay leaves

¼ generous teaspoon dried thyme

1 (14½-ounce) can chopped fire-roasted
tomatoes

2 tablespoons tomato paste

½ cup drained small pimento-stuffed
manzanilla olives (from a 5¾-ounce jar)

1 tablespoon drained capers

3 tablespoons chopped canned pickled
jalapeños plus 2 tablespoons pickling liquid

About ¼ cup all-purpose flour

2 pounds salt cod, soaked and prepped
(see note)

2 roasted red bell peppers, drained and sliced
into bite-size pieces (from an 8-ounce jar)

8 to 10 large rolls, preferably teleras,
Portuguese, kaiser, or ciabatta, split

About 6 tablespoons unsalted butter, softened

→ **MAKES 8 TO 10 ★**

Bacalao, or salt cod, is one of many Spanish ingredients taken up enthusiastically by Mexicans. Some people still call this preparation *a la vizcaína* after the province of Vizcaya in the Basque country, where it may have originated. Yet many call it *bacalao a la veracruzana* after the Mexican state of Veracruz, where it's enjoyed with particular enthusiasm, and to drive home that this version is thoroughly distinct from its Spanish antecedents.

Salt cod has become a popular item on the Christmas table. Even when there's ham, there's often bacalao, too. The day you make this simple stew, it goes well with rice or potatoes. It's the next day when people often make tortas from the leftovers, typically served with nothing more than rolls. I like to add a layer of pinto beans, a few avocado slices, and pickled jalapeño—an accessible substitute for the pickled *chiles güeros* (slim, yellow chiles) common as a bacalao topper in Veracruz.

→ **SOAKING AND PREPARING THE SALT COD:**
Cut the fish into 3 or 4 pieces and submerge in a large bowl filled with water. Soak the cod for 24 hours, changing the water four times, then drain the fish and pat it dry.

Cut the fish into approximately 4-inch pieces, then trim off any thick pieces of silvery skin and cut off and discard the floppy flaps.

MAKE THE SALT COD STEW:

★ Heat ¼ cup of the oil in a medium pot over medium-high heat until it shimmers. Add the onion and salt and cook, stirring, until the onion is softened and beginning to brown at the edges, about 8 minutes. Add the garlic, then add the bay leaves, thyme, tomatoes, tomato paste, olives, capers, and pickled jalapeños with the pickling liquid. Let it come to a steady simmer, adjust the heat to maintain the simmer, and cook, stirring occasionally, until the mixture thickens slightly, 15 to 20 minutes. Add 1 cup of water, reduce the heat to medium-low, and cover.

★ Meanwhile, put the flour in a bowl. Add the pieces of fish to the flour one at a time, turn to coat evenly, shake off the excess flour, and transfer the fish to a plate.

★ Heat the remaining ½ cup of olive oil in a medium saucepan over medium-high heat. When it's nice and hot (dip an edge of a piece of fish into the oil; the oil should bubble vigorously), fry the fish in batches, gently flipping once, until lightly golden on both sides, 4 to 5 minutes per batch. It's OK if the fish breaks into smaller pieces. As each piece is fried, use a slotted spoon to transfer it straight into the sauce, covering the pot after each addition.

★ Once all the fish is in the pot, gently stir to submerge the fish in the sauce. Cover and adjust the heat to maintain a very gentle simmer, stirring occasionally, until the flavors come together and the bacalao breaks into nice, big flakes, about 20 minutes. Stir in the peppers and continue simmering for 5 minutes. Season to taste with salt.

MAKE THE TORTAS:

★ Heat a large nonstick skillet over medium-high heat. Spread the butter evenly over the cut sides of the rolls. Cook the rolls, buttered sides down, in the skillet until they are light golden brown and crisp, but still soft in the middle, a minute or two.

★ If you'd like, spread a layer of **REFRIED PINTO BEANS**, homemade (page 148) or canned, over the roll bottoms. Add at least ½ cup of the salt cod to each sandwich, then top with **SLICED CANNED PICKLED JALAPEÑOS** and slices of **RIPE MEXICAN HASS AVOCADO**. Cover with the roll tops and press firmly but gently.

TORTAS with CHICKEN in GREEN MOLE
Tortas de pollo en pipián

¼ pound hulled raw (green) pumpkin seeds (¾ cup)

1 tablespoon plus 1½ teaspoons olive or vegetable oil

½ pound tomatillos (5 to 6), husked, rinsed, and coarsely chopped

4 fresh serrano or jalapeño chiles, stemmed, or more to taste

¼ medium white onion, coarsely chopped

2 medium garlic cloves, peeled

½ teaspoon dried Mexican oregano

¼ teaspoon cumin seeds

⅓ cup crumbled dried hoja santa leaves

1 teaspoon kosher salt

About 2½ cups low-sodium chicken stock

4 cups shredded chicken (from 1 rotisserie chicken)

About 4 tablespoons unsalted butter, softened

6 large rolls, preferably teleras, Portuguese, kaiser, or ciabatta, split

¾ cup Refried Black Beans or Refried Pinto Beans, homemade (page 148) or canned

→ **MAKES 6** ★

In Central Mexico, you can find tortas stuffed with chicken in mole poblano on virtually every corner. Eating the mole between bread is almost as common as having it beside rice and beans. Occasionally, you'll spot other moles and pipianes in tortas, even green pumpkin seed sauces, like this one from my friend and colleague Maria. Even without the fresh hoja santa and perfect pumpkin seeds she'd be able to buy in Guerrero, where she's from, she has figured out a way to make a stunningly good pipián with dried leaves and a little magic. The key is to make sure it's good and spicy—taste it after fifteen minutes or so of simmering, and if it's not hot enough, scoop some back into the blender and whiz it with another chile or two. All the garnishes are optional, except for the smear of beans, which insulates the roll from the saucy chicken.

→ **NOTE:** *These tortas are also fantastic on soft rolls, like challah or brioche, served in the style of marinas (page 86).*

MAKE THE PIPIÁN:

★ Preheat the oven or toaster oven to 350°F.

★ Spread the pumpkin seeds on a tray and toast them in the oven, shaking and tossing occasionally, until many of them have turned light brown, 3 to 5 minutes. Let them cool slightly, then add them to a blender (or even better, a spice grinder) and blend, poking and prodding them occasionally, to form a powder.

(Continued on page 82)

★ Heat the oil in a medium saucepan over medium heat until it just shimmers and stir in the pumpkin seed powder. It will clump up. This is a bit like cooking flour in butter to make a roux. Cook, stirring frequently, about 8 minutes.

★ Meanwhile, blend the tomatillos, chiles, onion, garlic, oregano, cumin, hoja santa, and salt along with 2 cups of the chicken stock until very smooth. Pour the blended mixture into the saucepan, stirring vigorously so the powder doesn't clump. Swish the remaining ½ cup of stock in the blender and pour it into the saucepan.

★ Raise the heat to bring the mixture to a gentle boil, then lower the heat to maintain a steady simmer. Partially cover the saucepan and cook, stirring occasionally and adding a little more stock or water if the pipián looks gloppy, until the pipián has thickened slightly and little pools of oil appear on the surface, 45 minute to 1 hour.

★ Stir the shredded chicken into the pipián. Lower the heat slightly and gently simmer uncovered until the pipián has thickened a bit more, 5 to 10 minutes. Season to taste with salt, up to ½ teaspoon more, depending on the saltiness of the chicken.

MAKE THE TORTAS:

★ Heat a large nonstick skillet over medium-high heat. Spread the butter evenly over the cut sides of the rolls. Cook the rolls, buttered sides down, in the skillet until they are light golden brown and crisp, but still soft in the middle, a minute or two.

★ Spread a layer of beans (a tablespoon or two) over the roll bottoms. Add at least ½ cup of the chicken to each sandwich, then top with SLICED CANNED PICKLED JALAPEÑOS, slices of RIPE MEXICAN HASS AVOCADO, and a pinch of salt. Cover with the roll tops and press firmly but gently.

➻ **PUMPKIN SEEDS:** *Mexican cooks use hulled, raw pumpkin seeds, which are small and pastel green, for cooking. You'll find them at many supermarkets and at your local natural foods store. Store them in an airtight container in a cool, dark place for two months and in the fridge for six months.*

TURKEY TORTA
Torta de pavo

☆ ☆

*About 3 tablespoons un-
salted butter, softened*

*4 large rolls, preferably
teleras, Portuguese, kaiser,
or ciabatta, split*

*½ cup Refried Pinto Beans
or Refried Black Beans,
homemade (page 148)
or canned*

*About 3 tablespoons
mayonnaise*

*4 teaspoons Dijon or yellow
mustard*

*Scant ¾ pound thinly sliced
smoked turkey*

*Generous ¼ pound sliced
Manchego cheese*

*8 or 12 slices crisp cooked
bacon*

→ **MAKES 4** ★

Everyone loves a good club sandwich, but imagine its pleasures—
the smoked turkey, the crunchy, salty bacon—revved up by those
of a Mexican torta. It's the best kind of fusion, an American classic
with a twist. Feel free to swap smoked turkey with slices of the fresh
meat leftover from Thanksgiving.

★ Heat a large nonstick skillet over medium-high heat. Spread
the butter evenly over the cut sides of the rolls. Cook the rolls, buttered sides down, in the skillet until they are light golden brown
and crisp, but still soft in the middle, a minute or two.

★ Spread a layer of beans (a tablespoon or two) over the bottom
half of each roll and spread the mayonnaise and mustard over the
roll tops. Stack the turkey, cheese, and bacon on the roll bottoms.
Top with SLICED CANNED PICKLED JALAPEÑOS, THINLY SLICED
WHITE ONIONS, slices of RIPE MEXICAN HASS AVOCADO, and a
pinch of salt. Cover with the roll tops and press firmly but gently.

YUCATÁN-STYLE PORK TORTAS
Tortas de cochinita pibil

☆ ☆ ☆ ☆ ☆ ☆ ☆ ☆ ☆ ☆ ☆ ☆ ☆ ☆ ★ ▲ ▲ ☆ ☆ ☆ ☆ ★ ☆ ☆ ☆ ☆ ☆ ☆ ☆ ☆ ☆ ☆ ☆ ☆ ☆

In the Yucatán, a mecca for the steaming heaps of orange-hued *cochinita pibil*, the tender pork is just as likely to be tucked into a roll as it is to be tonged onto tortillas. A slick of black beans and a handful of pickled red onions and you have a sandwich that tastes as if it came straight from a market in Mérida.

★ Heat a large nonstick skillet over medium-high heat. Spread the butter evenly over the cut sides of the rolls. Cook the rolls, buttered sides down, in the skillet until they are light golden brown and crisp, but still soft in the middle, a minute or two.

★ Spread a layer of beans (a tablespoon or two) on the bottom half of each roll and top with a generous ½ cup of the pork. Top the pork with a handful of the onions (still dripping in their pickling liquid). If you'd like, drizzle on **TOMATO-HABANERO SALSA** (page 128). Cover with the roll tops, and press firmly but gently.

About 3 tablespoons unsalted butter, softened

4 large rolls, preferably teleras, Portuguese, kaiser, or ciabatta, split

½ cup Refried Black Beans, homemade (page 148) or canned

1 recipe Yucatán-style pork (page 44), warm

Pickled Red Onions (page 147)

→ **MAKES 4** ★

MARINAS WITH MOLE
Marinas con mole

☆ ☆

1 medium tomato (½ pound), cored and very roughly chopped

¼ medium white onion, peeled, roughly chopped

2 medium garlic cloves, peeled

1 (8.25-ounce) jar Doña Maria brown mole

¼ cup light brown sugar

1 (½-inch) piece Mexican cinnamon

1 teaspoon white wine vinegar

1 teaspoon kosher salt

½ teaspoon chipotle powder (see page 210)

½ teaspoon ground cumin

¼ teaspoon dried thyme

⅛ teaspoon freshly ground black pepper

⅛ teaspoon ground clove

2 tablespoons olive or vegetable oil

3 cups shredded chicken (from 1 rotisserie chicken)

12 small brioche or challah rolls, split; or 12 hot dog buns, split

....
→ **MAKES 12** ★
....

When my family had friends over for the dinner-like late-afternoon meal Mexicans call *comida*, we'd serve these tiny, two-bite sandwiches on trays to our guests as a snack. My two favorite fillings for these treats are chicken in mole and Mexican chicken salad (page 88), the latter a take on the common tuna version, from which marinas probably get their name. The classic requires a particular small glossy roll, so here I call for small challah or brioche rolls, which are easy to find and quite similar.

〜〜〜〜〜〜〜〜〜

MAKE THE CHICKEN MOLE:

★ Put the tomato, onion, and garlic into the blender first, then add the next ten ingredients, along with 1½ cups of water. Blend until very smooth, about 1 minute.

★ Heat the oil in a medium pot over medium-high heat until it shimmers, then add the blended mixture, stirring constantly. Lower the heat to maintain a very gentle simmer and cook, stirring frequently, until the mole has thickened slightly, about 15 minutes.

★ Scoop out 1 cup of the mole and reserve it for another day (it keeps in the fridge for up to 5 days and in the freezer for up to a month). Stir the chicken into the mole in the pot and cook until it's warmed through. Season to taste with salt.

——— *Instead of insisting you make mole from scratch, here I've suggested doing what many cooks in the U.S. and Mexico do: Buy premade mole paste or powder and doctor it until it's nearly as tasty as the real deal. You can always use the mole as a filling for tacos, too, perhaps topped with crumbled queso fresco and strips of pickled jalapeño.*

☆ ☆ ☆ ☆ ☆ ☆ ☆ ☆ ☆ ☆ ☆ ☆ ☆ ☆ ★ ▲ ▲ ☆ ☆ ☆ ☆ ☆ ☆ ☆ ☆ ☆ ☆ ☆ ☆ ☆ ☆ ☆ ☆ ☆ ☆ ☆

MAKE THE MARINAS:

★ Heat a large nonstick skillet over medium heat. Place the rolls, cut sides down, in the skillet and cook until they are warm and barely colored, about 1 minute.

★ Scoop about ⅛ cup of the mole onto each roll bottom. Top with SLICED CANNED PICKLED JALAPEÑOS and thinly sliced WHITE ONION. Cover with the roll tops and press firmly but gently.

➡ **TORTAS DE MOLE:** *This mole is also fantastic in tortas de mole, more substantial sandwiches tricked out with the usual torta condiments: refried black beans, crema, avocado, pickled jalapeños, and the rest on a griddled roll.*

MARINAS WITH RUSSIAN SALAD
Marinas de ensalada rusa de pollo

☆ ☆

1½ cups diced (about ½-inch cubes) peeled waxy potatoes, like Yukon Gold

Kosher salt

1 cup diced (about ½-inch cubes) peeled carrots

1 cup frozen peas

2½ cups diced (about ¾-inch chunks) cooked chicken (from ½ rotisserie chicken)

⅓ cup finely chopped white onion

½ cup finely chopped celery

⅓ cup plus 1 tablespoon finely chopped canned pickled jalapeños

2½ tablespoons pickled jalapeño liquid

1 tablespoon Dijon mustard

⅓ cup mayonnaise

1 tablespoon freshly squeezed lime juice

¼ teaspoon freshly ground black pepper

24 small or 8 large brioche or challah rolls, split

→ **MAKES 24 SMALL OR 8 LARGE SANDWICHES ★**

This incredibly tasty chicken salad (what we in Mexico call Russian salad) is packed with mayo, vegetables, potatoes, and bright bits of pickled jalapeños. You'll love it, whether you serve it on small rolls as marinas or as Americans do chicken salad, on rye or whole wheat bread.

MAKE THE CHICKEN SALAD:

★ Put the potatoes in a small pot, add enough water to cover the potatoes by 1 inch, and add a generous handful of salt. Set the pot over high heat, bring the water to a boil, then lower the heat to maintain a gentle simmer. Cook just until the potatoes are tender and cooked through, about 5 minutes.

★ Use a slotted spoon or skimmer to remove the potatoes and transfer them to a colander to drain. Add the carrots to the water and cook at a vigorous simmer until they're tender with a slight crunch, about 7 minutes. Scoop them out of the water and transfer them to the colander with the potatoes. Cook the peas in the same way until they're tender, about 2 minutes, and drain them in the colander. Let the potatoes, carrots, and peas cool.

★ Combine the cooked vegetables with all the remaining ingredients in a large bowl, and stir gently but thoroughly. Chill the chicken salad for at least 1 hour.

MAKE THE MARINAS:

★ Heat a large nonstick skillet over medium heat. Place the rolls, cut sides down, in the skillet and cook until they are warm and barely colored, about 1 minute. Scoop about ⅓ cup of the salad onto each small roll bottom or ¾ cup onto each large roll bottom. Top with SLICED CANNED PICKLED JALAPEÑOS, then the roll tops, and serve.

GUADALAJARA-STYLE "DROWNED" TORTAS
Tortas ahogadas

☆ ☆

2 generous cups carnitas
(page 40)

4 large bolillos, split, or
1 large baguette, cut in
fourths, and split

Generous ½ cup Guadalajara-
Style Pickled Onions
(page 147)

About 1 cup Vinegary Árbol
Chile Salsa (page 142), at
room temperature

Generous 2 cups Simple
Tomato Sauce (page 92),
warmed

→ MAKES 4 ★

Perhaps the most famous tortas in Mexico and certainly one of the most unusual, *tortas ahogadas* are a must-try for anyone visiting the city of Guadalajara. Vendors first fill rolls called *birotes* with carnitas and a particular preparation of pickled onions, then dip the sandwich into a fiery, vinegary hot sauce—or as we say, the tortas are *bautisadas*, or "baptized." Some people order them half dipped (*media bautisada*) or fully dipped (*bautisada completa*). Then, vendors take a ladleful of mild tomato sauce from a vat and spoon it on top. It's a magical construction: crunchy and soggy, spicy and rich, pickly and mild.

More often than not, the tortas are cut into small pieces and served that way, a snack rather than a meal. But at home, I love to serve a whole sandwich per person, each in a shallow bowl to be eaten with a knife and fork, or with an enamel spoon as they do in Mexico. Guadalajara native Carmen Luz Sema taught me how to make *tortas ahogadas*, and I'll be forever grateful.

★ Heat a large skillet over medium heat. Add the carnitas and cook, stirring occasionally, until warmed through ands slightly crisp at the edges, about 5 minutes. Transfer the carnitas to a bowl and keep warm.

★ Place the bread, cut side down, in the same skillet and cook until it's warm and barely colored, about 1 minute.

★ Add a packed ½ cup of the carnitas to each roll bottom, top with 2 heaping tablespoons of the pickled onions, and cover with the roll tops. Put each sandwich in a shallow serving bowl. Over each sandwich, spoon 3 or so tablespoons of the árbol chile salsa, then a generous ½ cup of the tomato sauce. Serve with a knife and fork.

SIMPLE TOMATO SAUCE
Caldillo de tomate

☆ ☆

2 pounds ripe tomatoes (about 5 large), cored

1 tablespoon dried marjoram

Generous tablespoon kosher salt

3 tablespoons tomato paste, if necessary

1½ teaspoons sugar, if necessary

→ **MAKES 4 CUPS** ★

Meant to drown the Guadalajara-Style Tortas (page 90), this dead-simple, smooth, soupy tomato sauce also makes a tasty, mild accompaniment to fish or a braising liquid for chicken. The tomato paste and sugar are only necessary if you're forced to settle for mediocre tomatoes.

★ Put the tomatoes, core sides up, in a medium pot, and add enough water to come halfway up the sides of the tomatoes. Cover the pot and bring the water to a boil over high heat. Uncover the pot and lower the heat to maintain a simmer until the tomatoes are cooked all the way through, about 25 minutes.

★ Transfer the tomatoes to a blender jar, discarding the boiling liquid. Add the marjoram, salt, and, if necessary, the tomato paste and sugar. Blend until very smooth.

★ Strain the sauce through a sieve into a bowl, pressing and stirring to extract as much liquid as possible and discarding the solids. Swish 1 cup of water around in the blender jar and pour it through the sieve and into the bowl. Season with salt and sugar to taste.

★ **MAKE AHEAD:** The sauce keeps in the fridge for up to three days.

PUEBLA CITY-STYLE SANDWICHES
Cemitas

☆☆☆☆☆☆☆☆☆★☆ △ △ ☆☆☆☆☆▽▽☆☆☆☆☆☆☆☆☆☆☆

Named for the sesame seed roll it's served on, the *cemita* is a local take on the typical Mexican sandwich construction that you find in the city of Puebla. Besides that bread, what makes the sandwich a *cemita* is the addition of vinegary chipotles and *papalo*, a pungent herb with a distinctive flavor. But for the purposes of experiencing *a cemita* at home, any good roll will do. And if you can't find *papalo*, which is available in many Mexican markets, try mixing together 1 cup of tender cilantro sprigs with 1 cup of watercress, then tossing it with olive oil and a spritz of lime juice. It won't replicate *papalo*'s flavor, but it will provide a similarly welcome burst of herbaceousness.

~~~~~~

★ Heat a large nonstick skillet over medium-high heat. Spread the butter evenly over the cut sides of the rolls. Cook the rolls, buttered sides down, in the skillet until they are light golden brown and crisp, but still soft in the middle, a minute or two.

★ Spread a layer of beans (a tablespoon or two) over the bottom half of each roll and spread the crema over the roll tops. Add the chicken cutlets to the roll bottoms. Top with SHREDDED OAXACA CHEESE or SLICED QUESO FRESCO, PICKLED CHIPOTLES (page 146) or CANNED CHIPOTLES IN ADOBO, THINLY SLICED WHITE ONION, and slices of RIPE MEXICAN HASS AVOCADO. Cover with the roll tops and press firmly but gently.

About 3 tablespoons unsalted butter, softened

4 large cemitas or other rolls such as teleras, kaiser, Portuguese, or ciabatta, split

½ cup Refried Black Beans, homemade (page 148) or canned

¼ cup Mexican crema or crème fraîche, or 3 tablespoons mayonnaise

Chicken cutlets (page 74)

About 16 papalo leaves or a mixture of watercress and cilantro (see headnote)

→ **MAKES 4** ★

PACHOLA BURGERS
Hamburguesas estilo bisteces de metate

☆ ☆

1½ ounces guajillo chiles
(about 6), wiped clean,
stemmed, slit open,
seeded, and deveined

2 medium garlic cloves,
peeled

1 tablespoon apple cider
vinegar

1 tablespoon kosher salt

¾ teaspoon ground cumin

1 tablespoon plus 1 teaspoon
olive or vegetable oil

2 pounds ground beef
(preferably 20% fat)

½ cup finely diced red onion

½ cup lightly packed
chopped cilantro

5 large spearmint leaves,
finely chopped

4 large hamburger buns

....
→ **MAKES 4 ★**
....

Passing by hot dog vendor after hot dog vendor on the streets of New York City sometimes makes me wonder: in such a burger-crazy town, why can't you find carts hawking *hamburguesas*? Rather than sit-down sustenance, hamburgers in Mexico are mainly found in squares and road-side stalls. My version of this sizzling street treat is inspired by a Mexican dish called *pachola* or *bisteces de metate*, a patty of ground beef mixed with guajillo chile, garlic, and cumin—*not* served on a bun but instead alongside salsa, beans, and tortillas. Yet once it's grilled and topped with avocado slices and a drizzle of salsa or some pickled jalapeños, you have a burger that drowns out the memory of nearly all that came before it.

➡ **NOTE:** *For an even better burger, ask your butcher to grind the beef to order. My favorite lean-meat-to-fat ratio for burgers is 80% to 20%.*

MAKE THE PATTIES:

★ Soak the chiles in a bowl of cold water for 30 minutes, then drain well, discarding the water.

★ Combine the chiles with the garlic, vinegar, salt, cumin, and ¼ cup of fresh water in a blender and blend until very smooth, poking and prodding if necessary to get the chiles to blend. Don't be tempted to add more water.

★ Heat 1 tablespoon of the olive oil in a small pan over medium heat until it shimmers. Pour in the chile mixture, then swish 1 tablespoon of fresh water in the blender to get as much of the chile puree as possible. Pour it, too, into the pan.

★ Cook at a simmer, stirring constantly to prevent scorching, until the mixture thickens to the texture of tomato paste and the color turns slightly darker, 3 to 5 minutes. Let the chile puree cool completely.

(Continued on page 96.)

★ Combine the cooled chile sauce with the beef, onion, cilantro, and mint in a large bowl. Mix it all together with your hands until the ingredients are well distributed, no more than 30 seconds. Form 4 patties, each about ¾-inch thick.

MAKE THE BURGERS:

★ Rub a large heavy skillet (or the grates of a grill) with the remaining teaspoon of oil. Heat the skillet over medium-high heat until the pan smokes, then lower the heat to medium. Cook the patties until a deep brown crust forms on both sides and the burgers are cooked to your liking, 4 to 5 minutes per side for medium doneness. (Remember, the chile mixture gives the interior of the burgers a reddish color that shouldn't be mistaken for rare meat.) Transfer the patties to a plate to rest for 5 minutes.

★ Briefly toast the buns, if you'd like, top them with the burgers, and add slices of RIPE MEXICAN HASS AVOCADO, PICO DE GALLO WITH LEMON ZEST (page 127), and MEXICAN TARTAR SAUCE (page 149) or mayonnaise.

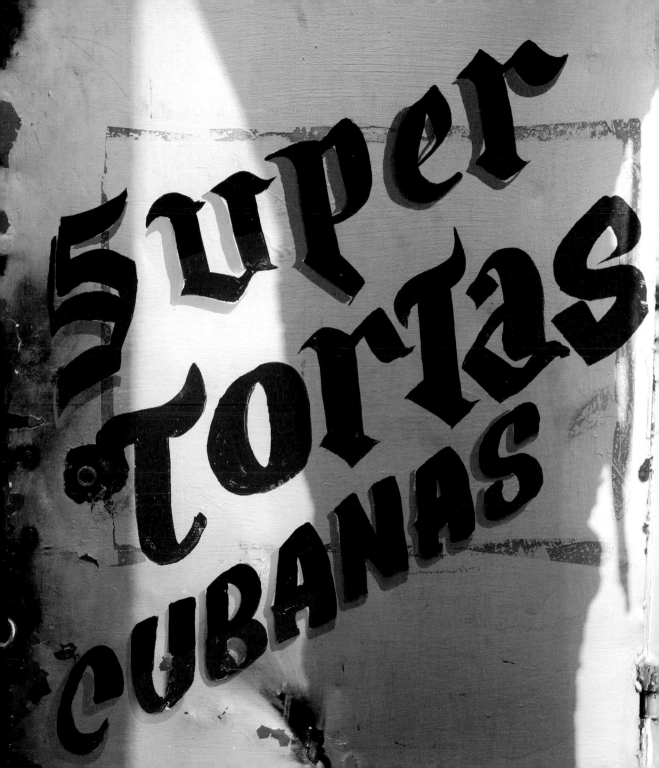

★ ★ ★

TAMALES

☆ ☆

IT'S FITTING THAT TAMALES often come wrapped like presents. Because what's inside when you peel back the corn husk or banana leaf is truly a gift. On the streets of Oaxaca City, that gift might be pillowy, savory dough encasing midnight-black mole. In the *zócalo* in D.F., you find simpler fillings like the charred strips of poblano chiles called *rajas* and a little cheese. Sometimes, you'll come across sweet tamales, their flavor the essence of corn or strawberries.

The wrapping that has become associated with the tamale is not in fact its defining feature. Derived from the word *nixtamal* (dried corn treated with slaked lime that's ground to make the masa used for tortillas, tamales, and other Mexican staples), the word *tamal* probably once referred to anything made from this nutritious corn mash. It was likely eaten with any number of other foodstuffs, just as tortillas are now, just another way of eating corn, of getting your daily sustenance. Even today, you'll find *tamales de cazuela* (page 117), polenta-like treats that are a window into the early form of tamales.

As you'd expect in a place as diverse as Mexico, tamales differ greatly throughout the country. This might mean the wrapping—the more familiar corn husk, for instance, gives way to the banana leaf in Oaxaca, oak leaves in the North, and large fresh avocado leaves in the countryside in the Volcanic Belt. The filling varies, too. In Oaxaca, you'll find tamales filled with the state's famous moles, like the pitch-black *mole negro* or golden *mole amarillo* (a fantastic way to use leftovers from the night before), while in Chiapas, the next state over, you might find tamales filled with prunes, capers, olives, and chicken cooked with saffron. Practically anything winds up inside—refried beans, shrimp, wild greens. In the city of Papantla, in Veracruz, I've seen locals gather to make a six-foot-long tamal wrapped in banana leaves (they call this leviathan *zacahuil*) and filled with all manner of things: hard-boiled eggs, pork, even whole chickens. The tamales steam in makeshift underground ovens all night long.

Even the masa itself changes as you travel throughout the vast country. In Oaxaca, you'll likely enjoy smooth, light, flan-like tamales made by cooks who strain masa so it's especially smooth, mix in plenty of lard, and simmer it until it thickens again. My mother adores sweet tamales, always stopping on the drive to visit my sister in Cuernavaca to buy pink ones made from masa mixed with butter and blackberries. My late grandmother used to make incredible *tamales de elote*, masa mixed with sweet corn, sugary enough to be dessert but served with a savory tomato sauce. There are even tamales that stretch the word's definition—I've unfolded banana leaves to find overstuffed tacos inside. Because tortillas are made of nixtamal, technically the creation can be called a tamal.

Today, tamales have a different place in Mexico City and other metropolises than they do in the countryside and small towns. In urban centers, you can get tamales just about anywhere. Before you reach the office, you'll almost certainly pass a woman presiding over a pot, her steamy packages awaiting a buyer. What a way to begin

☆ ☆

the day—a tamale and a cup of hot atole, the masa-thickened drink so often sold by the same vendors. Tamales, of course, are not just a morning meal, but an anytime snack, like bagels and pizza in New York City. Outside of cities, tamales are not as ubiquitous. They are first and foremost a food made at home—for birthdays and weddings, for reunions and other celebrations.

In fact, they make the perfect get-together food. I've spent many nights laughing with close friends as we all pitch in to fold corn husks around tamal dough. Sometimes, we set up a little assembly line—Lety spreads the masa onto the husks, I top it with simple pork and tomatillo stew, and Marco wraps each one. Once tamales go into the pot to steam, out comes the tequila. When guests arrive, we plunk the pot on the table and let them serve themselves. A salsa or two keeps lips tingling and the margaritas flowing. I can't imagine a better party.

In this chapter, you'll find one recipe for basic tamale dough with more than a dozen options for filling. In addition, there are several recipes for sweet tamales, one for a special tamale from Chiapas shared by a woman who has been making it for more than forty years, a recipe for the no-wrapping-required *tamal de cazuela*, and one for a fantastic casserole made from leftover tamales.

FILLINGS FOR TAMALES

Nearly anything delicious can serve as the filling for tamales, including many of the meat and vegetable options in the torta and taco chapters. Each tamal requires just a tablespoon or two of the filling, so for twenty-four tamales, you'll need two to three cups. Here are just some ideas:

➡ 2½ cups shredded chicken and Tomato-Habanero Salsa (page 128)

➡ ¾ pound goat cheese, diced; 12 canned pickled jalapeños, cut into strips; and 24 epazote leaves (optional)

➡ Refried beans (page 148)

➡ Rajas with bacon (page 27)

➡ Carnitas (page 40)

➡ Yucatán-style pork (page 44)

➡ Stewed frankfurters (page 70)

➡ Mushrooms (page 18) and Smoky Tomato Salsa (page 130)

➡ Cactus (page 24) and Tomatillo-Chipotle Salsa (page 134)

➡ Tomato-chipotle duck stew (page 33)

➡ Picadillo (page 53)

➡ Chicken in short-cut mole (page 86)

➡ Chicken in green mole (page 80)

WRAPPING TAMALES IN CORN HUSKS

Soak the corn husks in warm water for at least ½ hour. Drain well before using. You can keep the wrapped, uncooked tamales in the fridge for up to a day before steaming them. They'll take a little longer to cook if you steam them straight from the fridge.

FOR CLASSIC WRAPPING:

★ For each tamale, put about ⅓ cup batter in the center of the concave side of one corn husk. Spread to flatten it evenly so it forms a rough square. Put a tablespoon or two of the filling in the middle of the square.

★ Fold the long sides of the husk to enclose the filling in the batter, then fold the pointed end over the seam side. Put the package seam side down on another corn husk so that the open end of the package faces the pointed end. Fold the long sides of the second husk to enclose the package and fold the pointed end over the seam side. Turn the tamale over so the package stays closed. Repeat with the remaining batter, filling, and corn husks.

FOR "CANDY-WRAPPING":

★ Tear a few corn husks into long, thin strips for tying. You'll need two strips per tamale.

★ For each tamale, put about ¼ cup batter in the center of the concave side of one corn husk and spread to flatten it evenly so it forms a rough square.

★ Fold the long sides of the husk to enclose the filling in the batter, then one end at a time, gather the ends and tie each one tightly with a strip of husk to form a shape that looks like a large piece of candy. Repeat with the remaining batter, filling, and corn husks.

STEAMING TAMALES

The method for steaming tamales is the same for each version. Here's how to do it: fit the tamales in a dedicated tamale steamer or deep steamer basket of a pasta pot. Fill the pot with about 2 inches of water, and place a coin in the pot so you can tell if the water has evaporated (you will hear the coin start to jiggle when the water boils and you'll know you need to add more water when the jiggling noise stops). Bring the water to a boil.

Place the tamale-filled steamer basket in the pot, then cover the tamales with additional corn husks and a tight-fitting lid. (Covering the pot with two layers of heavy-duty foil, instead of a lid, will do, too.)

Steam the tamales, adding more boiling water if you no longer hear the coin jiggle, until you can easily and cleanly peel the husk from the tamal, about 45 minutes to 1¼ hours. Leave the tamales in the covered pot with the heat off for 15 minutes before serving.

BASIC TAMALES
Tamales

☆ ☆

10 ounces (1⅓ cups) golden-colored pork lard or vegetable shortening, chilled

5¾ cups tamale flour (masa harina para tamales)

Generous 2 tablespoons kosher salt

1½ teaspoons baking powder

6 cups Spice-Infused Water (see note) or room-temperature water

48 dried corn husks, soaked in warm water for ½ hour and drained well

2 to 3 cups filling (see options, page 102)

EQUIPMENT:
Stand mixer with whisk attachment

→ MAKES 24 TAMALES ★

★ Put the lard in the bowl of a stand mixer fitted with the whisk attachment. Beat the lard on high until it's white, fluffy, and tripled in volume (it'll look like vanilla icing), 7 to 8 minutes.

★ Meanwhile, combine tamale flour, salt, and baking powder in a large bowl and stir well. Add the water and mix well with your hands until you have a smooth dough. (The dough should be moist but not at all wet. If it's dry, very gradually knead in water.)

★ Lower the speed to medium-high and add the dough by the Ping Pong ball–sized piece until it's all added. Keep beating for another 5 minutes or so. To test that the batter is light and fluffy enough, fill a glass with water and drop in ½ teaspoon of the batter. If it doesn't sink rapidly to the bottom (or better yet, it floats), then you're ready to move to the next step. If not, keep beating.

★ Fill and steam according to the instructions on pages 102–103. They'll take about 45 minutes.

> ➥ **SPICE-INFUSED WATER:** *Combine* 2 TEASPOONS ANISEED, 2 TEASPOONS CUMIN SEEDS, *and* 10 TO 20 TOMATILLO HUSKS *with* 7 CUPS OF WATER *in a medium pot. Bring the water to a boil, cook for 10 minutes, then strain it into a large container. Measure 6 cups of the liquid (adding a little fresh water or pouring out a little water, if necessary). Let the liquid come to room temperature.*

TAMALES FROM CHIAPAS
Tamales chiapanecos

FOR THE FILLING:

Generous 6 tablespoons golden-colored lard or
mild olive oil

1 large white onion, diced

6 medium garlic cloves, finely chopped

5 dried árbol chiles, wiped clean and finely
chopped (including seeds)

2 cups crust-on bread (1-inch chunks),
toasted until deep golden brown and
crunchy throughout

1 teaspoon ground Mexican cinnamon

¾ teaspoon saffron threads

½ teaspoon freshly ground black pepper

⅛ teaspoon ground clove

1 (28-ounce) can fire-roasted whole tomatoes,
briefly pulsed in a blender to chunky puree

1½ teaspoons kosher salt

1 tablespoon plus 1 teaspoon sugar

1 cup low-sodium chicken stock

4 cups shredded chicken (from 1 rotisserie
chicken)

2 large red bell peppers

(Continued on page 108.)

Lucero Macal, whose family is from the state of Chiapas, lives next to my partner's parents in Mexico City. She prepares these unusual, wonderful tamales for friends as gifts and was kind enough to share her recipe with me. Inside each corn masa bundle, sweet raisins mingle with crunchy almonds and salty olives, the strong Middle Eastern influence on Mexican cuisine on full display. There's even saffron in the saucy chicken. I've adapted it, swapping local chiles for easier-to-find árbol chiles.

MAKE THE FILLING:

★ Heat the lard in a medium pot over medium heat until it shimmers. Add the onion, cook for 5 minutes, stirring occasionally, then add the garlic and árbol chiles. Cook for another 5 minutes, stirring, then add the bread, cinnamon, saffron, black pepper, and clove. Cook for 2 minutes, then add the tomatoes, salt, and sugar.

★ Let the tomatoes come to a simmer and adjust the heat to maintain a steady simmer, stirring frequently, until the mixture has thickened and has begun to stick to the pot, about 15 minutes. Add the chicken stock, cook at a steady simmer for 5 minutes, then add the shredded chicken. Cook until the sauce thickens to coat the chicken, about 8 minutes.

★ MAKE AHEAD: This can be made, covered, and refrigerated, up to two days in advance.

(Continued on page 108.)

FOR THE TAMALES:

1 package banana leaves, thawed if frozen, wiped clean on both sides, and cut into twenty-four 12×10-inch pieces, then toasted briefly over an open flame until very pliable

1 recipe Basic Tamale Dough (page 104)

1½ cups slivered almonds

1½ cups raisins

2 cups pimento-stuffed olives, sliced into thirds if large

→ **MAKES 24** ★

★ Turn one stove-top burner to high and roast the bell peppers on the racks of the burner (or directly on the element of an electric stove), turning frequently with tongs, until they are blistered and charred all over, 4 to 6 minutes. Put the peppers in a bowl and cover with a plate to sweat them for 15 to 20 minutes. Rub off the skin from the peppers (do not run them under water), then cut out the stems, seed pods, and veins, and lay the peppers flat. Wipe the peppers clean of seeds and cut the flesh into thin 2-inch-long strips.

MAKE THE TAMALES:

★ For each tamale, put about a generous ⅓ cup tamale dough in the center of a banana leaf piece and spread to flatten it evenly so it forms a rough square. Put ¼ cup chicken filling middle of the square leaving a ½-inch border. Add 1 tablespoon slivered almonds, 4 or 5 strips roasted pepper, 1 tablespoon raisins, and 1 tablespoon olives.

★ Fold the long sides of the leaf to enclose the filling in the batter, then fold shorter ends over the seam side. Turn the tamale over so the package stays closed. Repeat with the remaining banana leaves, dough, and filling. Steam the tamales according to the instructions on page 103. They'll take about 1 hour to cook.

TAMALES
ATOLES
* POZOLE
QUESADILL
PONC
TOSTA
P
FLAU

PASTOR-SUADERO
BISTEC
LONGANIZA
CAMPECHANO
GRINGAS
QUESADILLAS
SINCRONIZADA
AGUJAS (3)
ALAMBRES

STONE TAMALES
Tetamales

☆ ☆

1 pound piloncillo
(two 8-ounce pyramids),
coarsely chopped or grated

5 teaspoons aniseed

10 ounces golden-colored
pork lard or vegetable
shortening (1⅓ cups),
chilled

3½ cups tamale flour (masa
harina para tamales)

1½ teaspoons baking powder

1 generous tablespoon kosher
salt

½ pound chales, ground
(see note)

¾ cup small raisins

24 dried corn husks, soaked
in warm water for ½ hour
and drained well

EQUIPMENT:
Stand mixer with whisk
attachment

→ MAKES 22 TO 24 ★

These unusual sweet tamales from Mexico's Gulf Coast, flavored with anise and studded with raisins, were a specialty of my grandmother, one of the three varieties of corn-husk-wrapped treats that she'd make for us when I was little. From the Nahuatl word *tetl*, meaning "stone," their name refers to their shape (less oblong than round) and their deep brown color. Like that of any fine European cake, the secret to their deliciousness is sugar and fat, in this case, piloncillo and a combination of lard and *chales* (the crunchy bits left after cooking carnitas). They're rich and wonderful.

MAKE THE FILLING:

★ Combine the piloncillo and aniseed with ½ cup of water in a small pot. Set the pot over medium heat and bring it to a strong boil, stirring and breaking up the piloncillo until the piloncillo melts. Take the pot off the heat and use a spoon to smash any remaining chunks of piloncillo. Let the mixture cool to room temperature.

★ Put the lard in the bowl of a stand mixer fitted with the whisk attachment. Beat the lard on high speed until it's white and fluffy, like vanilla icing, 7 to 8 minutes.

★ Reduce the mixer speed to low and add the tamale flour, a cup or so at a time, and the baking powder and salt. Gradually increase the speed to medium and keep beating until the lard and tamale flour have been beaten together for about 5 minutes.

★ Add the chales and continue to beat on medium until well distributed, then add 2½ cups water, 1 cup or so at a time. Keep beating, stopping occasionally to scrape down the sides of the bowl, for about 10 minutes.

★ Pour in the cooled piloncillo mixture in a steady stream, and beat for about 3 minutes. Add the raisins and beat just until they're well distributed.

★ "Candy-wrap" and steam the tamales according to the instructions on page 103. They will take about 1 hour to cook.

→ **WHAT ARE CHALES?** *In Mexico, these crunchy, meaty pieces that settle to the bottom when cooking chicharrones and carnitas have many names— biuses, tlales, tlalitos, shish, and asiento, just to name a few. You'll find them in Mexican markets as a pebbly powder (you may have to do some searching, even if you live in L.A., San Francisco, or New York City). Occasionally, they will show up in small chunks. Either way, you'll need to grind them to a powder in a spice grinder. (I've even had success grinding them in a blender, though you end up with a paste, not a powder.) After grinding ½ pound of chales, you should have 1¼ cups of powder.*

STRAWBERRY TAMALES
Tamal de fresa

☆ ★ ★ ★ ▲ ▲ ▲ ▲ ☆

When my mom drives from Mexico City to my sister's house in Cuernavaca, she often stops along the way at a little shop devoted to tamales. She'll pick up a few dozen light, fluffy, sweet tamales, their doughs infused with the flavor of fruits like strawberries. These are just the thing to bring out as a special dessert at a dinner party. Traditionally, these tamales are dyed with cochineal, the little bug that provided the world with red coloring, but twenty drops of red food coloring will do the trick.

~~~~~~~~~~~~~~~~~~~~~~~~~~~~~~~~

★ Combine the strawberries, raspberries, sugar, vanilla extract, and orange zest in a medium saucepan. Set the pan over medium-high heat, let the mixture come to a strong simmer, and cook, stirring occasionally, until the berries are fully softened, 3 to 5 minutes. Transfer the mixture to a bowl, let it cool to room temperature, then blend it until very smooth.

★ Put the butter in the bowl of a stand mixer fitted with the whisk attachment. Beat the butter on high until it's white, fluffy, and tripled in volume (it'll look like vanilla icing), 7 to 8 minutes.

★ Combine the tamale flour and 2¼ cups of water in a large bowl and mix with your hands until you have a homogenous dough.

★ Reduce the mixer speed to low. Add the powdered sugar, baking powder, and salt to the butter, then mix on medium-high speed for 1 minute or so.

★ Alternately add the dough, 1 Ping-Pong ball–sized piece at a time, and some of the berry puree until you've added them all. Keep beating, occasionally scraping down the sides of the bowl, until the dough looks fluffy and light, 5 to 8 minutes. Add the dried cherries and food coloring, if using it, beating just until well incorporated.

★ "Candy-wrap" and steam the tamales according to the instructions on page 103. They'll take about 1 hour to cook.

Generous ¾ pound fresh ripe strawberries, tops removed and berries quartered (about 3 cups)

¼ pound ripe raspberries (1 scant cup)

1 cup sugar

1 tablespoon vanilla extract

2 teaspoons finely grated orange zest

2½ sticks unsalted butter, at room temperature

4 cups tamale flour (masa harina para tamales)

1 scant cup powdered sugar

1½ teaspoons baking powder

½ teaspoon kosher salt

1 cup dried cherries

20 drops red food coloring (recommended)

22 to 24 dried corn husks, soaked in warm water for ½ hour and drained well

EQUIPMENT:
Stand mixer with whisk attachment

....
➜ **MAKES 22 TO 24** ★
....

COCONUT TAMALES
Tamales de coco

☆ ☆

½ pound unsweetened shredded coconut (2½ cups)

1 tablespoon vanilla extract

2 sticks unsalted butter, at room temperature

3½ cups tamale flour (masa harina para tamales)

1 cup sugar

1 teaspoon baking powder

½ teaspoon kosher salt

¾ cup whole raisins, diced dried apricots, or roughly chopped dried cherries

22 to 24 dried corn husks, soaked in warm water for ½ hour and drained well

EQUIPMENT:
Stand mixer with whisk attachment

→ **MAKES 22 TO 24** ★

Here's another sweet tamale you'd find in Mexico. Try it for dessert or even for breakfast!

★ Combine the coconut and vanilla extract with 1 cup of water in a medium bowl. Soak, stirring occasionally, until the coconut softens slightly, about 20 minutes.

★ Put the butter in the bowl of a stand mixer fitted with the whisk attachment. Beat the butter on high until it's white, fluffy, and tripled in volume (it'll look like vanilla icing), 7 to 8 minutes.

★ Meanwhile, combine the tamale flour and 2½ cups of water in a large bowl and mix with your hands until you have a homogenous dough.

★ Reduce the mixer speed to medium-low and add the sugar, baking powder, and salt, then increase the speed to medium-high.

★ Alternately add the dough, 1 Ping-Pong ball–sized piece at a time, and some of the coconut mixture until you've added them all. Keep beating, occasionally scraping down the sides of the bowl, until the dough looks fluffy and light, about 8 minutes.

★ Add the dried fruit to the dough and beat just until well distributed.

★ "Candy-Wrap" and steam the tamales according to the instructions on page 103. They'll take about 1 hour to cook.

TAMAL COOKED IN A CAZUELA
Tamal de cazuela

This one-pot dish is a home-cook classic, the flavor of tamales without all that wrapping. The dough, made from a combination of grits and tamale flour to replicate the hominy masa used in Mexico, can be layered with any tasty, not-too-liquidy filling. The banana leaves lining the pot add flavor to the dish and make for a beautiful presentation, but parchment paper works, too. Serve a little salsa on the side.

★ Combine the stock, grits, and tamale flour in a medium pot and bring the mixture to a boil over medium-high heat, stirring frequently. Lower the heat to maintain a simmer, and cook, stirring frequently, until the mixture has thickened slightly, about 10 minutes. Stir in the lard and continue cooking until you have a mixture that's the texture of thick porridge, about 10 minutes more. Stir in the salt.

★ Preheat the oven to 350°F. Heat a large skillet over high heat until it just begins to smoke. One by one, toast the banana leaf pieces in the skillet for about 20 seconds per side. This brings out their aroma and makes them more pliable.

★ Lay 2 of the banana leaf pieces perpendicularly in an 8- to 9-quart ovenproof Dutch oven or deep baking dish, pressing lightly with your hands so they line the bottom and sides to create a little nest.

★ Spread a layer of masa (about 2 cups, depending on the size of your pot) into the pot, then spread a layer of the filling over the masa. Repeat, using all the masa and filling and ending with a final layer of masa. (If your filling isn't highly seasoned, season each layer generously with salt.)

★ Fold the visible banana leaves over the tamal as best you can, then cover with the remaining piece of banana leaf, tucking it between the dough and the sides of the pot to make a neat bundle.

★ Cover the pot with a tight-fitting lid or aluminum foil and cook in the oven until the tamal is steaming hot all the way through, 1 to 1½ hours. Let it sit for 15 to 20 minutes, then serve.

8 cups low-sodium chicken stock

1 cup quick-cooking hominy grits

1 cup tamale flour (masa harina para tamales)

½ cup golden-colored lard or vegetable oil

1 teaspoon kosher salt

3 banana leaf pieces (each about 16×12 inches), thawed if frozen (optional)

Mushrooms (page 18), Yucatan-Style Pork (page 44), Picadillo (page 53), or Chicken with Poblanos and Tomatoes (see page 118)

→ **SERVES 8 TO 10 AS MAIN DISH** ★

CHICKEN WITH POBLANOS AND TOMATOES

☆ ☆

1 pound fresh poblano chiles (about 3 medium)

2 pounds tomatoes (about 5 medium), cored

½ medium red onion, cut into ½-inch-thick round slices

4 cups shredded chicken (from 1 rotisserie chicken)

24 medium epazote leaves, coarsely chopped (optional)

¾ teaspoon kosher salt

This mixture makes a great filling for Tamal de Cazuela (page 117) and Basic Tamales (page 104).

★ Roast, peel, seed, and slice the poblanos according to the instructions on page 116.

★ Meanwhile, preheat the oven to 500°F. Put the tomatoes, cored sides up, on a large, foil-lined baking sheet and roast them in the oven until they are blackened and cooked to the core, 20 to 30 minutes.

★ Heat a medium skillet over medium-low heat. Lay the onion slices in the pan and cook, turning them over occasionally, until they are softened and charred on both sides, 15 to 25 minutes. Transfer them to a cutting board.

★ Coarsely chop the onion. Peel and cut the tomatoes into pieces. Reserve the tomato juice that's released for another purpose.

★ Between each layer of masa (see page 117), add a layer of the poblanos, tomatoes, onion, chicken, epazote leaves (if using them), and a generous sprinkle of salt. You'll have enough for about three layers of filling.

TAMALE CASSEROLE
Budín de tamales

☆ ☆

Leftover tamales, either homemade or purchased from your favorite vendor, are an exciting prospect when you have this wonderfully sloppy casserole in your repertoire. My recipe should serve more as guidance than instruction, because virtually every component is up to you. I love the combination of gooey cheese, rich cream, lip-tickling tomato salsa, and smoky roasted poblano chiles. But you can use any salsa, skip the cheese, and use shredded chicken or even meat left over from adobos and moles!

★ Preheat the oven to 350°F.

★ In a medium casserole dish, layer the tamale pieces, poblano strips, salsa, crema, and cheese, finishing with a layer of cheese, until you've used them all.

★ Cover the dish tightly with aluminum foil and bake until bubbling hot, 45 minutes to 1 hour. Remove the foil, let the casserole sit for 5 to 10 minutes at room temperature, and serve.

10 large tamales (about 7 ounces each), remove and discard husks and cut into about 2×1-inch chunks

4 large fresh poblano chiles, roasted, peeled, seeded, and cut into strips (see page 16)

1½ cups Smoky Tomato Salsa (page 130)

About 1 cup Mexican crema or crème fraîche

About 10 ounces shredded Chihuahua, Monterey Jack, or cheddar cheese

→ SERVES 6 ★

★ ★ ★ ★

SALSAS
and condiments

☆ ☆

IN MEXICO, SALSA IS NOT ONE THING, but many. Its diversity in Mexico today might surprise anyone who associates the word with jarred to-mato mush. *How odd!* I remember thinking when I first arrived in the U.S., and saw Americans dip into this stuff with chips as an appetizer.

Rather than a dip for chips, salsa is primarily an assertively seasoned condiment meant to add spark to whatever it touches—a mound of meat, a bowl of soup, a plate of rice or beans, a sand-wich. Every country has its condiments, yet no-where but Mexico are the arrows in this culinary quiver at once so numerous and varied and yet so ingeniously simple. In this chapter, you'll find a variety of salsas, both traditional and modern, as well as condiments such as simple pickles and even highly seasoned beans meant to provide a similar palate pick-me-up.

In the U.S. today, diners new to salsas often assume there are two kinds: green and red. Yet these colors are actually just broad categories in and of themselves. For example, many green-colored salsas you see are made with tomatillos. But the similarities end there—to name just a few, there's the bright, verdant *salsa verde cruda*, raw tomatillos whizzed in a blender with chiles, garlic, onions, and cilantro; there are pulpy khaki-green, tangy versions made with roasted tomatillos and dried chiles like chipotles; and there are smooth pastel-green sauces blended with avocado that tread the line between salsa and guacamole. I re-member a visit as a child to the town of Tlayacápan

in the state of Morelos, where I ate tomatillo salsa seasoned with chile and *jumiles*, a local insect that we bought live at the market. Its almost bacony, umami-rich flavor is etched in my memory.

Plus there is a seemingly infinite spectrum of salsas beyond green and red, including sweet-tart *salsa negra* from Veracruz, a deep purple, almost black puree that's as thick as brownie dough. In the center of the country, where maguey plants thrive, people drink the fermented sap, a viscous alcoholic beverage called *pulque*, that provides the unique flavor, along with the pasilla chiles com-mon in the region, to *salsa borracha* ("drunken" salsa). The pungent but relatively mild sauce is eaten with barbacoa, slow-cooked lamb or goat.

The astoundingly diverse battery that devel-oped is a testament to the country's astounding cultural and geographic diversity—high plains and coasts, deserts and dense jungles. What is now Mexico once comprised groups of indigenous peoples with completely different cultures and languages. Dozens of languages are still spoken today, and many culinary traditions have endured the conquest and modernity.

Here's the good news: unlike moles, the cat-egory of rich sauces made with vegetables, fruits, nuts, and seeds that has saddled Mexican cuisine with a reputation as being elaborate and labor-intensive, salsas demonstrate how the country's cooks create intense, exhilarating flavor with just a few ingredients. Learn to make even a few and your dinners will never be the same again.

→ **HOT STUFF** *Use caution when blending hot mixtures, because the steam that collects in the jar can cause the lid to pop off and send liquid flying. To avoid this, either let the mixture cool slightly before blending, blend in small batches, or rapidly pulse the mixture, remove the lid to let the steam out, cover again, and then blend as normal.*

WHAT SALSA MEANS TO ME

What drew me to my favorite street vendors in Mexico was, of course, the skill with which they fried, grilled, or stewed, but most memorably, it was the thrill of the salsas they served.

As a high-school kid, I adored a particular quesadilla stand, nameless and probably long gone. I had great affection for the quesadillas, sure, but mainly I loved the brick-red mixture the proprietor set out in a *cazuelita* on her rickety folding table. When I visited my favorite carnitas vendor, I was excited for a mouthful of pork, braised and then fried in its own fat, but also for bright-green salsa verde cruda that I'd spoon liberally on top, which cut through the richness of the meat with its prickly heat and bracing acidity like a knife through a ripe mango.

At home in Mexico City, there was always salsa on our table, either next to warm tortillas and our housekeeper Marta's inimitable beans or beside crusty bread and glasses of red wine. Even when my grandmother cooked pasta timbale to please my grandfather—a very European Mexican, always dressed in a suit, tie, and hat, who refused to eat tortillas—I could not resist adding a drizzle.

Perhaps the most regular presence at our home table was *salsa roja de molcajete*, a dead-simple concoction that embodies Mexican cooking. The three main ingredients—tomato, chile, and garlic—could very well produce an Italian sauce but for the distinctive way Mexicans treat them. Instead of a pan of hot olive oil, the process begins on the flat pan called a comal and there's no oil in

sight. Tomatoes and serrano chiles slowly blister and blacken, sending up an incredible smell, a little sweet and beguilingly bitter. It's an aroma that defined my early life, an aroma I took for granted until I left Mexico and it became a vivid reminder of home.

More than a decade ago, when I first arrived in New York City, where I live today, I was alone in a new country. I missed my family terribly. And as much as I loved eating Pakistani food one day and Chinese or French or Polish the next, I missed the electricity of the food in Mexico, of the life I left behind. Even as I took my first bite of exquisitely cheesy pizza, like some mammoth, otherworldly quesadilla, I craved that bolt of flavor, the spark that set my mouth ablaze with spiciness (often enough to make the top of my head tingle) and thrilled me with the combination of saltiness, sweetness, and acidity.

Today, however, I've integrated salsa into my everyday eating and you can, too. The salsas in this chapter go fantastically with Tacos (pages 7–55), Tortas (pages 57–97), and Tamales pages 99–119), but you don't have to make an entire Mexican meal in order to enjoy them. My life, like everyone's, is a manic mixture of friends and work and family. I return to my apartment each night, often too late and too exhausted to cook. On the way, I might grab a rotisserie chicken or turkey sandwich. I'll pop a few tomatoes and chiles into my toaster oven, broiling them as I read my mail until they blacken and blister. I'll mash the roasted chiles with garlic and salt to a paste and then mix in the roasted tomatoes. I'll take a sniff. Now I'm home.

→ **THE SECRET TO GREAT SALSA** *Salsa is not about moderation. Just a small streak is meant to add thrilling spark to whatever it touches, not to be slurped by the spoonful or heaped on tortilla chips. So please resist the temptation to hold back on tartness, saltiness, and spiciness when seasoning your salsas. Keep in mind that the heat of chiles, especially fresh ones, varies greatly, so always buy a few more than you think you'll need, in case you need to adjust the spice level. Also keep in mind that the heat level will dip an hour or so after you make a salsa.*

ROASTED CHERRY TOMATO SALSA
Salsa de tomatitos

This riff on the classic *salsa roja* makes use of consistently sweet cherry or grape tomatoes. I roast them to intensify their flavor, then slip off their skins and toss the fleshy little orbs with chile, garlic, and a few other ingredients to create a vibrant condiment that's great on just about anything.

2 pints cherry or grape tomatoes

3 fresh serrano or jalapeño chiles, stemmed, or more to taste

2 medium garlic cloves, peeled

1½ teaspoons kosher salt

2 tablespoons freshly squeezed lime juice, or more to taste

¼ cup chopped cilantro

¼ cup finely diced white onion

Generous drizzle extra-virgin olive oil

★ Preheat the oven to broil or 500°F.

★ Put the tomatoes on a large foil-lined baking sheet and roast them under the broiler or in the oven until they are softened and blackened in spots, 10 to 15 minutes. Remove the tomatoes from the oven and let them cool slightly.

★ Meanwhile, preheat a dry pan over medium-low heat. Roast the chiles in the pan, turning occasionally, until they're blistered all over and blackened in spots, about 15 minutes. Slip the skins from the tomatoes, and use a paring knife to gently scrape the skin from the chiles.

★ Pound the garlic with the roasted chiles and salt to a paste in a molcajete or other mortar. Alternatively, you can mince and mash the ingredients together on a cutting board with a fork or large knife, and then transfer the paste to a bowl.

★ Add the tomatoes to the chile mixture and gently stir so they're well coated in the paste. Add the lime juice, cilantro, and onion, and drizzle in the olive oil. Stir once more, and season to taste with more chile, lime juice, or salt.

★ MAKE AHEAD: You can make this salsa up to 12 hours before you plan to serve it.

→ **MAKES ABOUT 2 CUPS** ★

PICO DE GALLO WITH LEMON ZEST

Pico de gallo con limón amarillo

Pico de gallo, also known as *salsa mexicana*, has become a common sight on tables in the U.S., and it's easy to see why. The highly-seasoned mixture of raw, chopped ingredients improves just about any meal with its lively acidity, lip-tingling heat, and crisp texture. This version swaps the classic lime for lemon to great effect. Whenever I take a bite I have a heretical thought: This is so delicious that maybe we Mexicans should use only lemons!

~~~~~~~~~~~~~~~~~~~~~~~~~

1½ cups diced seeded tomatoes

⅓ cup finely chopped red onion

Heaping ¼ cup chopped cilantro

2 teaspoons finely grated lemon zest

2 tablespoons plus 1 teaspoon freshly squeezed lemon juice, or more to taste

1½ tablespoons finely chopped fresh serrano or jalapeño chiles (including seeds), or more to taste

1½ teaspoons kosher salt

★ Combine all the ingredients in a large bowl and stir thoroughly. Season to taste with more chile, lemon juice, and salt. I like to let the salsa sit for at least 30 minutes before serving.

★ MAKE AHEAD: You can make this salsa up to a few hours before you plan to serve it.

→ **MAKES ABOUT 2 CUPS**

PICO DE GALLO WITH ÁRBOL CHILES

Pico de gallo con chiles de árbol

In another take on the classic, I substitute the classic jalapeño or serrano chiles with fresh árbol chiles. They bring a different sort of heat, one that hits you at the end rather than the beginning of each bite. Of course, feel free to use the more typical chiles, if you'd like, as long as you keep in mind the principles of great pico de gallo: Make sure the salsa is seasoned aggressively with salt, citrus, and chiles.

~~~~~~~~~~~~~~~~~~~~~~~~~

1¼ cups diced seeded tomatoes

⅓ cup chopped cilantro

Heaping ¼ cup finely chopped white onion

3 fresh green árbol chiles, including seeds, finely chopped, or more to taste

2 tablespoons freshly squeezed lime juice, or more to taste

1½ teaspoons kosher salt

★ Combine all the ingredients in a large bowl and stir thoroughly. Season to taste with more chile, lime juice, or salt, if you want. I like to let the salsa sit for at least 30 minutes before serving.

★ MAKE AHEAD: You can make this salsa up to a few hours before you plan to serve it.

→ **MAKES ABOUT 2 CUPS**

GUANAJUATO-STYLE PICO DE GALLO

Pico de gallo estilo guanajuato

A must in any Guanajuato-Style Carnitas Torta (page 76) and Guacamaya (page 77), this salsa combines the freshness and crunchy texture of pico de gallo with the palate-invigorating sharp spiciness of dried árbol chiles. While the condiment deserves its own recipe, I've come up with a very close approximation made from two salsas already included in this book!

2 cups Pico de Gallo with Lemon Zest (page 127)

¾ cup Vinegary Árbol Chile Salsa (page 142)

Kosher salt

★ Combine the salsas in a bowl, stir well, and season to taste with salt.

★ MAKE AHEAD: You can make this salsa up to a few hours before you plan to serve it.

→ MAKES ABOUT 2¾ CUPS ★

TOMATO-HABANERO SALSA

Chiltomate para tacos

1½ pounds tomatoes (about 5 medium), cored

2 to 3 fresh habanero chiles, stemmed

¼ medium white onion, roughly chopped

1 small garlic clove, peeled

1¾ teaspoons kosher salt

2 tablespoons olive or vegetable oil

★ Preheat the oven to broil or 500°F.

★ Put the tomatoes, cored sides up, on a large foil-lined baking sheet and roast until the tops have blackened and the tomatoes are cooked to the core, 20 to 30 minutes.

★ Preheat a pan over medium-low heat. Roast the chiles until they're softened and blackened in spots, 8 to 12 minutes.

★ Peel the tomatoes, then puree the tomatoes, habaneros, onion, garlic, and salt in a blender until smooth.

★ Heat the oil in a medium saucepan over medium heat. Add the tomato mixture and gently simmer, stirring occasionally, until the flavors have come together, about 10 minutes. Let cool and season to taste with salt.

★ MAKE AHEAD: This salsa keeps in the fridge for up to three days or in the freezer for up to one month.

→ MAKES ABOUT 2 CUPS ★

GUANAJUATO-STYLE PICO DE GALLO

SMOKY TOMATO SALSA
Salsa ranchera para tacos

Two very different chiles, the dried chipotle and the fresh habanero, lend their flavor and fire to this salsa. The result is smoky and bright, tinged with sweetness, and irresistible on Tacos of Roasted Poblanos and Cream (page 16), Mushroom Tacos (page 18), and Marinated Skirt Steak Tacos (page 47), among so many others.

1½ pounds tomatoes (about 5 medium), cored

2 dried chipotle mora chiles (small, purplish-red), wiped clean and stemmed

1 small fresh habanero chile, stemmed

1 large garlic clove, peeled

1 teaspoon kosher salt

¼ teaspoon sugar

½ cup finely chopped white onion

1 (½-inch) piece Mexican cinnamon

2 tablespoons mild olive or vegetable oil

★ Preheat the oven to broil or 500°F.

★ Put the tomatoes, cored sides up, on a large foil-lined baking sheet and roast until their tops have blackened and the tomatoes are cooked to the core, 20 to 30 minutes.

★ Meanwhile, preheat a small dry pan over medium-low heat. Cook both types of chiles in the pan, turning them over occasionally, until the chipotles have puffed up and blistered in spots, 3 to 5 minutes, and the habanero has softened and blackened in spots, 8 to 12 minutes.

★ Peel the tomatoes, then puree the tomatoes in the blender with the chiles, garlic, salt, and sugar until very smooth.

★ Heat the oil in a medium heavy saucepan over medium heat. Cook the onions and cinnamon, stirring, until the onion is translucent, about 5 minutes. Pour in the blended tomato mixture and simmer, stirring occasionally, until the sauce has thickened slightly, about 10 minutes. Let cool and season to taste with additional salt or sugar.

★ MAKE AHEAD: This salsa keeps in the fridge for up to three days or in the freezer for up to one month.

→ MAKES ABOUT 2 CUPS ★

HABANERO SALSA WITH CREAM
Salsa de habanero con crema

This luxurious salsa is my invention: a rich, velvety puree with the sneaky, warm heat of habanero. It goes great with just about anything—a drizzle over fish or chicken would be a fine dinner indeed. But what will really blow your guests away is my Duck Tacos with Habanero-Cream Sauce (page 36), tender duck rolled in tortillas and coated with this salsa, like enchiladas.

2 large red bell peppers (about 1 pound)

1 medium-large tomato (about 9 ounces), cored

1 small fresh habanero chile, stemmed

1 tablespoon olive or vegetable oil

½ medium white onion, coarsely chopped

3 medium garlic cloves, peeled

8 whole allspice berries

1½ cups heavy cream

1½ teaspoons kosher salt

★ Turn one stovetop burner to high and roast the bell peppers on the rack of the burner (or directly on the element of an electric stove), turning frequently with tongs, until they are blistered and charred all over, 4 to 6 minutes. Put them in a bowl and cover with a plate for 20 minutes. Rub off the skin from the peppers (do not run them under water), then cut out the stems, seed pods, and veins, and lay the peppers flat. Wipe clean and discard the seeds.

★ Meanwhile, preheat the oven to broil or 500°F. Put the tomato, cored side up, on a foil-lined baking sheet and roast until the tomato is blackened and cooked to the core, about 25 minutes.

★ Preheat a dry small pan over medium-low heat. Roast the habanero in the pan until it has softened and blackened in spots, 8 to 12 minutes.

★ Heat the oil in a deep pan over medium-high heat until the oil shimmers. Add the onion, garlic, and allspice and cook, stirring occasionally, until the onion is translucent, about 5 minutes. Roughly chop the bell peppers, tomatoes, and habanero, and add them to the onion mixture. Cook, stirring, for 5 minutes, then add the cream and salt. Bring the mixture to a simmer, cook for 5 minutes more, then turn off the heat.

★ Working in batches to avoid blending with a full jar, carefully blend the mixture until it is very smooth.

★ Use the warm salsa right away, or let cool completely and rewarm it over low heat.

★ MAKE AHEAD: This salsa keeps in the fridge for up to three days.

→ MAKES ABOUT 4 CUPS ★

FRESH GREEN SALSA

FRESH GREEN SALSA

Salsa verde cruda

Tart and fiery, this classic bright-green salsa shows off the flavor of tomatillos and the lovable grassy sharpness of fresh unripe chiles. Serve it with anything that would benefit from lively contrast, such as rich Carnitas Tacos (page 40).

→ **AVOCADO POWER!** *Want a more velvety version with the same thrilling flavors? Just double the amount of chiles, bump up the salt by ½ teaspoon, add ½ cup water, and scoop in the flesh of a large, ripe Hass avocado before you blend.*

½ pound tomatillos (5 or 6), husked, rinsed, and coarsely chopped

½ cup coarsely chopped cilantro

2 fresh jalapeño or serrano chiles, coarsely chopped (including seeds), or more to taste

1 large garlic clove, peeled

2 tablespoons chopped white onion

1½ teaspoons kosher salt

★ Put the tomatillos in a blender first, then add the remaining ingredients. Pulse a few times, then blend until the salsa is very smooth, at least 1 minute. Season to taste with additional chile and salt, and blend again.

→ **MAKES ABOUT 1½ CUPS ★**

AVOCADO-TOMATILLO SALSA

Salsa de aguacate y tomatillo

This is the sort of salsa you'll find in the plastic jars perched on the counters on many a modest taqueria or fastened to a mobile operation selling *tacos de canasta*, or "basket tacos." It's rustic, chunky, and hot!

½ pound tomatillos (5 or 6), husked and rinsed

3 fresh serrano or jalapeño chiles, stemmed

1 small garlic clove, peeled

1¼ teaspoons kosher salt

½ cup finely chopped white onion

1 small, ripe Mexican Hass avocado, pitted, peeled, and chopped into 1-inch chunks

½ cup chopped cilantro

★ Combine the tomatillos and chiles in a small pot and add enough water to cover (they'll float; that's fine). Bring the water to a boil over medium-high heat and cook, stirring occasionally, until the tomatillos are a khaki color and soft to the core, about 5 minutes. Gently drain and discard the water.

★ Combine the tomatillos, chiles, garlic and salt in a blender and pulse until you have a coarse puree. Pour the mixture into a serving bowl, let cool slightly, then stir in the onion, avocado, and cilantro. Season to taste with salt.

→ **MAKES ABOUT 1 CUP ★**

TOMATILLO-CHIPOTLE SALSA

Salsa de tomatillo y chipotle

Tomatillos and chipotles make such great partners, and the tangy, spicy product is just the thing to complement grilled meats. Instead of asking you to find, clean, and toast dried chipotle chiles, I came up with a recipe that uses easy-to-find canned chipotles without any sacrifice in smoky flavor.

½ pound tomatillos (5 to 6), husked and rinsed

3 canned chipotle chiles in adobo, including a little adobo liquid

2 teaspoons kosher salt

1 medium garlic clove, peeled

1 tablespoon freshly squeezed lime juice

★ Preheat the oven or toaster oven to broil or 500°F.

★ Put the tomatillos on a foil-lined baking sheet and roast them, turning them over once, until their tops and bottoms have blackened and the tomatillos are cooked to the core, 20 to 30 minutes. Let them cool slightly.

★ Blend the roasted tomatillos with the remaining ingredients until very smooth. Season to taste with more salt and lime juice.

★ MAKE AHEAD: This salsa keeps in the fridge for up to three days.

→ MAKES 1 CUP ★

TOMATILLO-ÁRBOL SALSA

Salsa de tomatillo y chile de árbol

Tangy roasted tomatillos and nutty árbol chiles make a fine team in this fiery salsa, along with the last-minute additions of crunchy onions and fresh cilantro.

½ pound tomatillos (5 or 6), husked and rinsed

2 tablespoons olive or vegetable oil

15 unbroken dried árbol chiles (½ ounce), stemmed and wiped clean

1 medium garlic clove, peeled

1¼ teaspoons kosher salt

2 tablespoons finely chopped white onion

2 heaping tablespoons chopped cilantro

★ Preheat a medium pan over medium-high heat. Cook the tomatillos, turning over once, until they are blackened on their tops and bottoms but not cooked to the core, about 10 minutes. Put them in a blender.

★ Heat the oil in a small pan over medium heat until the oil shimmers. Add the chiles and cook, stirring constantly, until they are very deep brown, about 2 minutes. Add the chiles and the oil in the pan to the blender along with the garlic, salt, and ¼ cup of water. Pulse until you have a coarse puree.

★ Let cool completely, then mix in the onion and cilantro, plus salt to taste.

★ MAKE AHEAD: This salsa keeps in the fridge for up to three days.

→ MAKES 1¼ CUP ★

TOMATILLO-ÁRBOL SALSA

JALAPEÑO AND PINEAPPLE SALSA
Salsa de jalapeños con piña

My friend and star assistant Maria Barrera, who shared and helped test recipes for this book, grew up in the mountains of Guerrero eating this salsa at home and at her cousin's taco stand in the town of Tlapa. Savory and spicy, the salsa also provides sweetness with every chunk of pineapple. The addition of chicken stock, common in Guerrero, adds a welcome richness.

6 ounces fresh serrano or jalapeño chiles, roughly chopped (including seeds)

⅓ cup finely chopped white onion

2 small garlic cloves, peeled

1 cup low-sodium chicken stock

¾ cup diced (¼-inch) cored peeled pineapple (about ¼ ripe pineapple)

¼ cup olive or vegetable oil

1¼ teaspoons kosher salt

★ Blend the jalapeños, onion, garlic, and most of the chicken stock until smooth, then pour the mixture into a small saucepan or pot. Swish the remaining stock in the blender, then pour it in too.

★ Add the pineapple, oil, and salt, set the pan over medium-high heat, and bring the mixture to a boil. Boil for a minute or so, stirring frequently. Pour it into a bowl and let it cool completely. Season to taste with salt.

★ MAKE AHEAD: This salsa keeps in the fridge for up to three days.

→ MAKES 2½ CUPS ★

FRIED CHILE SALSA
Salsa de chile frito

No roasting required here. You simply cook vegetables and chiles in oil and blend it all until the salsa has a smooth, emulsified texture, almost like mayonnaise. But unlike mayonnaise, the flavor is explosive, a combination of wicked spiciness and tanginess that you won't soon forget.

➡ **NOTE:** *It's important to use more or less unbroken chiles for this salsa, and as you stem them, be careful not to break them. You don't want the seeds to escape into the hot oil, because they may burn.*

¼ cup olive or vegetable oil

2 medium garlic cloves, peeled

¼ medium white onion (2 ounces), thinly sliced

2 whole cloves

1 ounce unbroken dried árbol chiles (30 to 40), stemmed

½ pound tomato (1 medium), cored and cut into 8 wedges

2 tablespoons apple cider vinegar

1½ teaspoons kosher salt

½ teaspoon sugar

★ Heat the oil in a medium pan over medium heat until it shimmers, then add the garlic cloves and cook, turning them over occasionally, until they are golden brown all over and soft, about 4 minutes. Use a slotted spoon to transfer the garlic to a blender.

★ Raise the heat to medium-high. Add the onion to the pan and cook, stirring occasionally, until the onion is soft, about 4 minutes. Add the cloves and cook until the onion is golden brown at the edges, about 2 minutes. Use a slotted spoon to transfer the onion and cloves to the blender with the garlic.

★ Add the chiles to the same pan and cook over medium-high heat, tossing gently, until very fragrant and a shade or two darker, about 1 minute. Use a slotted spoon to transfer the chiles to the blender. Finally, add the tomato wedges to the pan and cook, turning them over occasionally, until they are cooked through and very soft, 5 to 7 minutes.

★ Transfer the tomatoes and the liquid remaining in the pan to the blender, then add the vinegar, salt, sugar, and ½ cup of water.

★ Blend until the salsa is very smooth, about 2 minutes. Let cool completely. Season to taste with salt.

★ **MAKE AHEAD:** This salsa keeps in the fridge for up to a week.

➡ **MAKES ABOUT 2 CUPS ★**

PECAN-CHIPOTLE SALSA
Salsa de nuez con chipotle

I envy anyone who has yet to taste this amazing salsa, because I remember my first bite and the wonderful surprise it brought. Rich pecans and smoky chipotles partner to create a mouth-filling salsa with slow-building heat. Taco-friendly, for sure, to be spread on the tortillas before topping them with meat, its texture is even better suited to being slathered onto bread for simple tortas.

3 dried chipotle mora chiles (small, purplish-red), wiped clean and stemmed

½ cup pecans, coarsely chopped

2 tablespoons olive or vegetable oil

½ cup finely chopped white onion

1 medium garlic clove, finely chopped

½ teaspoon kosher salt

★ Preheat a dry small pan over medium-low heat and toast the chiles, turning them over occasionally, until they've puffed up and blistered in spots, 3 to 5 minutes. Transfer them to a blender along with ½ cup of water.

★ Preheat the oven to 350°F and toast the pecans in one layer on a baking sheet, shaking once or twice, until they're about two shades darker and very fragrant, 5 to 8 minutes. Transfer them to the blender. Blend the mixture to form a slightly chunky puree, gradually adding more water if necessary to blend.

★ Wipe the small pan clean, add the oil, and set the pan over medium heat. When the oil shimmers, add the onion and garlic and cook just until the onion is translucent and soft, about 2 minutes. Add the blended mixture to the pan, then pour 1 tablespoon of water into the blender to loosen the remaining puree and pour it into the pan.

★ Add the salt and let the mixture come to a strong simmer, stirring constantly, then turn off the heat. Let the salsa cool, then season it to taste with more salt.

★ MAKE AHEAD: This salsa keeps in the fridge for up to five days.

→ MAKES ABOUT 1 CUP ★

VINEGARY ÁRBOL CHILE SALSA

Salsa de chile de árbol

This vinegary, incendiary liquid, perhaps a predecessor of Tabasco, is one of the salsas into which *tortas ahogados* (page 100) are dipped. If you're not planning to make those fabulous *tortas*, use it as a homemade hot sauce.

~~~

2 ounces dried árbol chiles (about 65), stemmed and rinsed

½ cup distilled white vinegar

3 medium garlic cloves, peeled

20 whole black peppercorns

3 whole cloves

1 teaspoon crumbled dried marjoram

1½ teaspoons kosher salt

⅛ teaspoon ground cumin

★ In a small pot, bring the chiles and enough water to cover to a boil and simmer, stirring occasionally, until the chiles are very soft, 15 to 20 minutes.

★ Drain the chiles and transfer to a blender with the remaining ingredients and ½ cup of water. Blend until very smooth, at least 2 minutes.

★ Strain the sauce into a bowl, pressing and stirring to extract as much liquid as possible.

★ MAKE AHEAD: This salsa keeps in the fridge for up to one week.

→ MAKES 1½ CUPS ★

FRESH GUAJE SALSA

Salsa de guajes frescos

Purchased in little bundles in many Mexican markets, guajes are flat pods filled with small green seeds. These seeds—eaten as a snack and turned into all manner of sauces—have a striking flavor that's slightly funky, vegetal, and, if you know what I mean, very *green*. My talented friend and kitchen colleague Maria whipped up this version (just three ingredients!) that she used to make as a young woman in Guerrero and that really showcases the guajes' flavor. It tastes especially amazing with eggs and beef.

→ **PEELING GUAJES:** *Lay each pod flat, run a sharp knife along the edge of the pod but not through the seeds, and then separate the two layers.*

~~~

30 to 40 guaje pods, peeled

2 fresh serrano or jalapeño chiles, coarsely chopped (including seeds)

1 heaping tablespoon chopped cilantro

1 teaspoon kosher salt

★ Discard any seeds that are mushy. Measure ½ cup of seeds and blend them with the chiles, cilantro, salt, and ½ cup of water to a slightly coarse puree. Season to taste with salt.

★ MAKE AHEAD: This salsa keeps in the fridge for up to three days.

→ MAKES ¾ CUP ★

FRESH GUAJE SALSA

ANGRY CHILES
Chiles toreados

In the bullfighting ring, a matador tries to make a bull (*toro*, in Spanish) mad enough to charge at him. What he aims to do is *torrear*, or provoke, the bull, to make it angry. That's what you do to the chiles in this recipe. You agitate them with your hands, then roast them so they're especially spicy. The lip-tingling thrill also comes with a mouthwatering quality provided by a dose of lime juice, Worcestershire sauce, and soy sauce. One taste and you'll understand why Mexico City residents adore this cosmopolitan condiment, often found in Japanese restaurants as well as people's homes.

➡ **TRY THIS!** *I love to use* chiles toreados *to top simple tacos of shredded rotisserie chicken, the warm tortillas slathered with mayonnaise. Despite what you might think (soy sauce and mayonnaise?), this combination of flavors is so very Mexican!*

12 fresh serrano or very small jalapeño chiles

1½ tablespoons olive or vegetable oil

1 medium white onion, thinly sliced
    into half-moons

¼ teaspoon kosher salt

2 tablespoons Worcestershire sauce

A scant 2 tablespoons soy sauce

¼ cup freshly squeezed lime juice
    (from 2 juicy limes), or more to taste

★ Preheat a dry shallow pan over medium heat until it is hot but not smoking. Firmly roll each chile between your palms for a few seconds, but be careful not to break them. Put the chiles in the pan and cook, turning them over occasionally, until they're blistered all over and blackened in spots, 10 to 15 minutes.

★ Transfer the chiles to a bowl. Add the oil, onion, and salt to the pan and cook, stirring, until the onion is tender and golden brown at the edges, about 5 minutes.

★ Turn off the heat, add the chiles back to the pan, and poke each chile once with the tip of a sharp knife, so the chiles release a little juice. Add the Worcestershire sauce, soy sauce, and lime juice, and stir well.

★ Transfer the mixture to a bowl (if you'd like it even spicier, pluck out the chiles, coarsely chop them, and stir them back into the mixture). Let it sit for at least 5 minutes. Season to taste with more salt and lime.

★ **MAKE AHEAD:** This mixture keeps in an airtight container in the fridge for up to three days.

➡ **SERVES 4 TO 6** ★

PICKLED CHIPOTLES

Chipotles en vinagre (chipotles escabechados)

In the states of Puebla and Veracruz, these fragrant, tangy, fiery chipotles are as common as canned chipotles in adobo are elsewhere. Virtually every corner store has them, and many cooks make their own, like my friend Ana Elena, whose recipe inspired mine. They're indispensable to true Cemitas (page 93), they're excellent alongside anything from rice and beans to grilled steak (try mincing a few of the chiles, mixing them with a couple of tablespoons of the liquid, and adding that to your next sandwich!), and they'll keep in the fridge for up to two months.

---

12 dried chipotle mora chiles (small, purplish-red), wiped clean and stemmed

4 cups apple cider vinegar

3 tablespoons olive or vegetable oil

1 medium white onion, thinly sliced into half-moons

6 dried bay leaves

2 teaspoons dried Mexican oregano

1 teaspoon dried thyme

1 tablespoon kosher salt

4 medium garlic cloves, peeled

½ generous cup grated piloncillo (about 2 ounces), or ½ cup lightly packed brown sugar

★ Combine the chipotles and vinegar in a medium pot. Set it over medium-high heat, bring to a boil, and cook for 10 minutes, turning over the chiles occasionally. Cover the pot, let the mixture cool completely, then refrigerate it overnight.

★ Heat the oil in a large pan over medium heat until it shimmers. Add the onion, bay leaves, oregano, thyme, and salt and cook, stirring, for 3 minutes. Add the garlic and cook until the onion is translucent, about 3 minutes more.

★ Add the chipotles and vinegar, and stir in the piloncillo. Let the mixture come to a steady simmer, adjusting the heat to maintain the simmer, and cook just to bring the flavors together, about 8 minutes. Let it cool.

★ Pour the mixture into a large container, preferably a glass jar. You can eat the chipotles right away, but they taste even better after two weeks.

★ MAKE AHEAD: The pickled chipotles keep in an airtight container in the fridge for up to two months.

→ MAKES 12 PLUS SEVERAL CUPS PICKLING LIQUID ★

PICKLED RED ONIONS

Cebollas rojas encurtidas

These pretty pink pickles are the typical topper for Yucatán-style pork (page 44), yet they're great to have around any time you need a tart, crunchy accompaniment. Don't neglect the flavorful liquid in which the onions wade.

20 whole black peppercorns

8 whole allspice berries

1 whole clove

½ generous teaspoon dried Mexican oregano

1 medium red onion (about 9 ounces), thinly sliced into half-moons

¾ teaspoon kosher salt

¼ cup distilled white vinegar

¼ cup freshly squeezed lime juice (from 2 to 3 juicy limes)

★ Pound the peppercorns, allspice, clove, and oregano in a mortar to a coarse powder. Put the onion in a medium bowl, and add the spice mixture and the salt. Use your hands to firmly scrunch and massage the onion, tossing as you do. Add the vinegar and lime juice, and toss well.

★ Transfer the mixture to a narrow, straight-sided container, cover, and store in the fridge for 24 hours. Give the container an occasional shake.

★ MAKE AHEAD: The pickled red onions keep in the fridge for up to five days.

→ MAKES ABOUT 2 CUPS ★

GUADALAJARA-STYLE PICKLED ONIONS

Cebollas desflemadas de Guadalajara

Like pickled red onions, these are meant for a particular purpose—in this case, *tortas ahogadas* from Guadalajara (page 90)—but I adore them scattered on just about any sandwich.

1 small white onion (about 8 ounces), very thinly sliced into half-moons

¾ teaspoon dried marjoram

2 tablespoons distilled white vinegar

¼ cup freshly squeezed lime juice (from 2 to 3 juicy limes)

1¼ teaspoons kosher salt

★ Combine all the ingredients in a medium bowl. Stir well, then transfer the mixture to a narrow, straight-sided container. Cover and let the mixture sit overnight or, even better, for 24 hours in the fridge, stirring and tossing once.

★ MAKE AHEAD: The pickled onions keep in the fridge for up to five days.

→ MAKES 1¾ CUPS ★

REFRIED PINTO BEANS

Frijoles pintos refritos

A layer of these flavor-packed beans is essential to many tortas. I'll also serve them with eggs in the morning and, for that matter, in place of standard beans in almost any situation.

~~~~~~~~~~~~~~~~

2½ bacon slices, sliced crosswise into ¼-inch-wide pieces

¼ cup finely chopped white onion

1 (15½-ounce) can pinto beans, including liquid

¼ teaspoon chipotle powder, homemade (page 210) or purchased

⅛ teaspoon dried Mexican oregano

⅛ teaspoon ground cumin

★ Put the bacon in a cold pan and set it over medium-high heat. Cook, stirring occasionally, until the bacon browns and threatens to crisp, about 8 minutes. Add the onion, and cook, stirring and scraping, until it softens, about 3 minutes. Add the beans, the chile powder, oregano, and cumin.

★ Let the beans come to a brisk simmer, then lower the heat to maintain a gentle simmer. Cook, stirring and mashing, until the beans resemble a very coarse puree and have thickened, 10 to 15 minutes. The beans will thicken a little more once they cool. Add salt to taste. Use warm or at room temperature.

★ MAKE AHEAD: They keep in the fridge for up to five days.

→ MAKES ABOUT 1½ CUPS ★

REFRIED BLACK BEANS

Frijoles negros refritos

Another fantastic substitute for soupy beans, these pack a punch, which is just the thing for tortas. The chile powder should be reduced by half if serving these beans as a side dish.

~~~~~~~~~~~~~~~~

2 tablespoons olive or vegetable oil

⅓ cup finely chopped white onion

1 (15½-ounce) can black beans, including liquid

1 medium garlic clove, pressed or finely grated

½ teaspoon árbol chile powder (page 210) or cayenne pepper

★ Heat the oil in a medium pan over medium-high heat until it shimmers. Add the onion and cook, stirring often, until it's soft and browned at the edges, about 5 minutes. Add the beans, garlic, and chile powder.

★ Let the beans come to a brisk simmer, then lower the heat to maintain a gentle simmer. Cook, stirring and mashing often until the beans resemble a very coarse puree and have thickened, 15 to 20 minutes. When you tip the pan, the beans should creep forward like lava. The beans will thicken a little more once they cool. Add salt to taste. Use warm or at room temperature.

★ MAKE AHEAD: They keep in the fridge for up to five days.

→ MAKES ABOUT 1¼ CUPS ★

MEXICAN TARTAR SAUCE
Salsa tartara

I just love to slather this creamy, crunchy, spicy sauce on shrimp and fish, either tucked into tacos or just piled on a plate.

~~~~~~~~~~

½ cup mayonnaise

¼ cup finely chopped drained dill pickles

3 tablespoons finely chopped drained canned pickled jalapeños

2 tablespoons finely chopped red onion

1 teaspoon Dijon mustard

½ teaspoon freshly ground black pepper

★ Combine the ingredients in a bowl and stir until the ingredients are well distributed. Season to taste with salt.

★ MAKE AHEAD: The sauce keeps in the fridge for up to two days.

→ MAKES 1 CUP ★

CREAMY AVOCADO SAUCE
Salsa de aguacate

Guanajuato-Style Carnitas Tortas (page 76) require a particular condiment, which this sauce mimics nicely. Of course, you'll find yourself slathering the silky avocado puree on any sandwich you dream up.

~~~~~~~~~~

½ large, ripe Mexican Hass avocado, pitted

½ cup whole milk, or more if necessary

1 fresh serrano or jalapeño chile, coarsely chopped (including seeds)

½ small garlic clove, peeled

½ teaspoon kosher salt

2 tablespoons chopped cilantro

★ Scoop the avocado flesh into a blender and add the milk, chile, garlic, and salt. Blend until smooth, silky, and thick but still drizzle-able, gradually blending in more milk, if necessary. Season to taste with the salt, then add the cilantro and pulse just until it's well distributed.

★ MAKE AHEAD: Press a piece of plastic wrap directly onto the surface of the sauce and refrigerate the sauce for up to two hours. Let it come to room temperature before serving.

→ MAKES ABOUT 1 CUP ★

★ ★ ★

DRINKS

☆ ☆

AFTER A DAY UNDER THE SCORCHING MEXICAN SUN, there's nothing like a cool drink. And boy, are you in the right country. Just about everywhere you look, people are set up behind giant jugs filled with brightly colored drinks called *aguas frescas*. There's red watermelon, bright-yellow pineapple, and stunning green limeade, among so many others, each tasting like a liquid version of ripe fruit. Some markets and street stalls make fantastic drinks called *licuados*, essentially smoothies made with a little milk and dairy-friendly fruits like papaya, mango, and strawberry.

Fruit isn't the only thing we turn into beverages. Agua de jamaica, for example, is made from dried hibiscus flowers steeped in water, wine-colored and tangy. There are even drinks made of ground seeds, nuts, and grains, likely born as yet another way to wrest nutrients from nature's bounty. Fresh almond and rice milks become *horchata*, fragrant from Mexican cinnamon. Masa, the corn dough from which tortillas and tamales are made, and amaranth flour thicken *atoles* sold by vendors who also sell tamales. Keep your eyes peeled and you'll spot fruit-flavored atole, chocolate-spiked atole (known as *champur-*

rado), and even *chile atole*, a savory drink made from chiles and herbs like epazote and hoja santa. Like drinkable oatmeal, they fortify you in the morning and fill you up for the light dinner called *merienda*.

As anyone who's spent time with my friends and me can attest, we Mexicans do enjoy a tequila or three, as well as the spirit's small-batch cousin, mezcal. That's not to mention ancient alcoholic beverages like *tepache* and *pulque*, made respectively from fermented pineapple rinds and agave sap (and not included in this book). While the margarita has become the iconic cocktail, I also adore *toritos*, the Veracruzana concoctions made from fruit, sometimes other ingredients like peanuts, and *agua ardiente* (literally translated as "ardent water"), a sugarcane-based spirit with a mild flavor similar to French eau-de-vie or Italian grappa. And *micheladas*, beer made even more refreshing thanks to additions like lime juice and chile, are perfect for a day at the beach or late breakfast after one too many the night before.

This chapter is devoted to just some of the incredible drinks you'd sip on the streets, in markets, or at a table beside a bustling square.

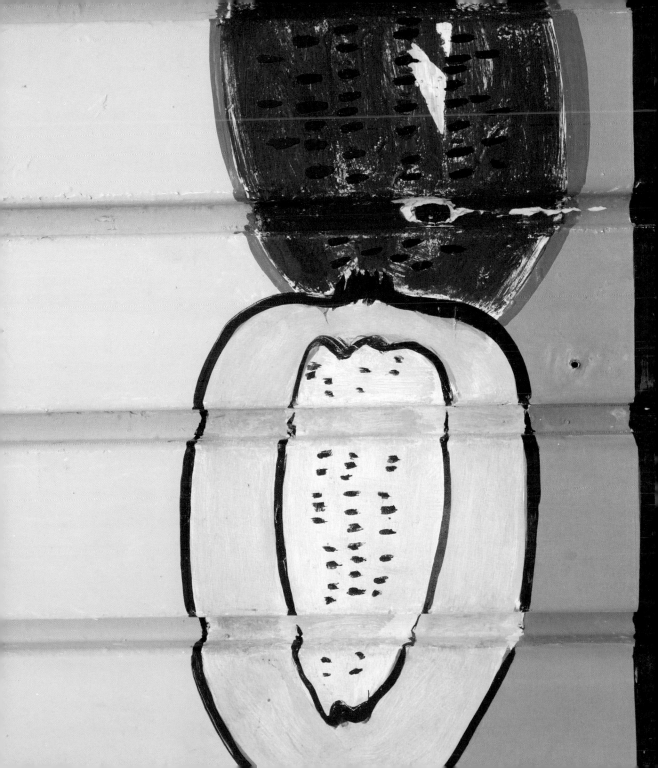

TIPS FOR MAKING AGUAS

☆ ☆

★ Making great aguas is all about getting a feel for your fruit. Sweeter fruit will need less sugar. Especially tart fruit might need less lime juice. You're aiming for a sweet, but not unnaturally sweet, drink balanced occasionally by a hint of lime juice's tartness. Always taste your fruit and season the drink to taste, though keep in mind that the flavor will dilute slightly once the drink is poured over ice. Always add sugar before you add ice—otherwise, the sugar won't fully dissolve.

★ Most aguas are best made just a few hours before you plan to drink them. Cover the pitcher and refrigerate. Because these drinks are made with real fruit, there will be a little sediment, so always stir right before serving.

★ If your blender isn't large enough to handle the amount of water I call for in some of the recipes, either blend in batches or blend with some of the water, then add the rest after blending and straining.

★ If I have any fruit left over, I like to use it to garnish the drink, floating a small handful of raspberries in the pitcher or perching pineapple pieces on the rim of each glass.

MEXICAN LIMEADE
Agua de limón

On a hot day, I urge you to try this Mexican classic instead of lemonade. It may seem odd at first to blend the limes whole, but the result is delightful. The skin adds a striking fragrance and the slightly bitter pith balances the drink's sweetness. Just don't make it more than an hour or so in advance, as the pith will turn the drink too bitter.

2 limes, rinsed well, quartered, and seeds flicked out

¼ cup sugar

Ice cubes

★ Combine the limes (yes, skin and all!) and sugar in a blender along with 3 cups of water. Blend until very smooth, then strain through a sieve into a large pitcher.

★ Season to taste with sugar. Stir thoroughly, pour the limeade into ice-filled glasses, and drink immediately.

→ **MAKES 4 LARGE TALL, ICY GLASSES**

HIBISCUS AGUA FRESCA
Agua de jamaica

Vendors standing beside giant jars filled with this dazzling wine-red drink always stop me in my tracks. Because inside could be nothing but this tangy delight—essentially a cold, sweetened hibiscus-flower tea. I provide a range for the sugar, though I bet most Mexicans would prefer the version made with the full cup.

→ **NOTE:** *I like to reserve a small handful of the soaked flowers and add them to the pitcher with the agua when I'm ready to serve it. The purplish flowers look strange and beautiful, and you can eat them, too.*

2 cups (about 3 ounces) dried hibiscus flowers

¾ to 1 cup sugar

Ice cubes

★ Bring 4 cups of water to a boil in a medium pot. Add the hibiscus flowers, turn off the heat, cover the pot, and let the flowers steep for 20 to 30 minutes.

★ Strain the mixture through a sieve into a large pitcher, pressing on the flowers to extract as much liquid as possible, then discarding the solids. Add the sugar and stir until it dissolves. Pour in 5 cups of water, stir, and season to taste with sugar.

★ Chill the pitcher in the fridge, then pour the agua fresca into ice-filled glasses or refrigerate for up to three days.

→ **MAKES 8 TALL, ICY GLASSES**

PINEAPPLE AGUA FRESCA

PINEAPPLE AGUA FRESCA

Agua de piña y hierba buena

Sweet-tart pineapple and fresh spearmint make for a brightly flavored beverage that would be the life of any party.

~~~~~~~~~~~~~~~~

2 cups ripe 1-inch pineapple chunks

⅓ cup sugar

8 large spearmint leaves

Up to ¼ cup freshly squeezed lime juice, if necessary

Ice cubes

★ Blend the pineapple, sugar, and mint along with 3 cups of water until very smooth.

★ Strain the pineapple mixture through a sieve into a large pitcher, smashing the solids to force out as much juice as you can. Stir in 1 cup of water. Gradually season the agua fresca to taste with more sugar and lime juice.

★ Chill the pitcher in the fridge, then stir thoroughly and pour the agua fresca into ice-filled glasses.

→ **MAKES 6 TO 8 TALL, ICY GLASSES**

CUCUMBER AGUA FRESCA

Agua de pepino

Mexicans love cucumbers, both as spears dipped in salt and chile powder or in sweet preparations like this one. This pretty pale-green drink is tremendously refreshing and will convert anyone who doubts that cucumbers benefit from a little sugar.

~~~~~~~~~~~~~~~~

1 English cucumber (about ¾ pound), peeled and roughly chopped

½ cup sugar, or more to taste

¼ scant cup freshly squeezed lime juice

Spearmint sprigs for garnish (optional)

Ice cubes

★ Blend the cucumber, sugar, and lime juice with 3 cups of water until very smooth.

★ Strain the mixture through a sieve into a large pitcher, then stir in 1 cup of water. Gradually season the agua fresca to taste with sugar and lime juice.

★ Chill the pitcher in the fridge, then stir thoroughly, add the mint sprigs, if using them, and pour the agua fresca into ice-filled glasses.

→ **MAKES 6 TO 8 TALL, ICY GLASSES**

WATERMELON AGUA FRESCA

Agua de sandía

Few things are as refreshing as cold chunks of sweet watermelon. Well, I know one thing that is—a chilled, chuggable beverage full of the same luscious flavor. Don't fret over stray seeds. They'll break up in the blender and you'll remove them once you strain the liquid.

*6 cups cubed ripe watermelon
(about 1½ pounds), seeds flicked out*

*½ cup freshly squeezed lime juice
(from about 4 juicy limes)*

¼ cup plus 3 tablespoons sugar

Ice cubes

★ Work in two batches to blend the watermelon with the lime juice and 1 cup of water total until the mixture is smooth and the sugar has completely dissolved, about 30 seconds. Strain the mixture into a large pitcher, pressing on then discarding the solids. Pour in 4½ cups of water, and stir well. Season to taste with sugar.

★ Chill the pitcher in the fridge, then stir thoroughly and pour the agua fresca into ice-filled glasses or refrigerate for up to a day.

→ MAKES 6 TO 8 TALL, ICY GLASSES

RASPBERRY AGUA FRESCA

Agua de frambuesa

Whether you use fresh summer raspberries or frozen ones, you'll have a crowd-pleasing, rose-colored agua that tastes like summer in the *zócalo*.

*1 generous cup fresh or frozen raspberries
(6 ounces)*

¼ cup sugar

3 tablespoons freshly squeezed lime juice

Ice cubes

★ Blend the raspberries, sugar, and lime juice with 3 cups of water until very smooth. Strain the mixture through a sieve and into a large pitcher.

★ Chill the pitcher in the fridge for at least an hour or up to 24, then stir thoroughly and pour the agua fresca into ice-filled glasses and serve immediately.

→ MAKES 4 TO 5 TALL, ICY GLASSES

PINEAPPLE, LIME, AND SPINACH AGUA

Agua de piña con alfalfa y limón

When I was a kid, my parents had a country house in Morelos, near the town of Yautepec. We drove there from Mexico City, and our first stop was a nameless *licuaderia*. There, as at almost all *licuaderias*, the counterman blended fresh fruits to order and strained the mixture straight into your cup. My mom would order us a drink of her creation: a little pineapple, whole lime, and a small handful of alfalfa greens. The alfalfa was a funny addition, perhaps her attempt at counteracting the generous scoop of sugar that also went into the drink with something healthful.

Today, I like to hold back a little on the sugar, but I know my Mexican friends would nudge me to add another ¼ cup. So feel free to blend in more sugar to taste before pouring the drink over ice. And instead of alfalfa greens, which are virtually impossible to find in the U.S., I add a handful of baby spinach.

½ cup chopped ripe pineapple

1 juicy lime, rinsed well, quartered, and seeds flicked out

1 small handful baby spinach (about ½ lightly packed cup)

¼ cup sugar

Ice cubes

★ Combine the pineapple, lime (yes, skin and all!), spinach, and sugar in a blender with 3 cups of water. Blend until very smooth, then strain through a sieve and into a large pitcher.

★ Gradually season the agua fresca to taste with sugar and stir thoroughly, then pour the agua fresca into ice-filled glasses and serve immediately.

→ **MAKES ABOUT 4 LARGE TALL, ICY GLASSES**

STRAWBERRY-LIME AGUA FRESCA

STRAWBERRY-LIME AGUA FRESCA

Agua de fresa y limón

Here, lime lends its bracing tartness to the fragrant sweetness of strawberries. If you can't find perfectly ripe, in-season strawberries, try adding a touch of vanilla extract to duplicate the aroma.

~~~

1 pound ripe strawberries, hulled

⅓ cup sugar

¼ cup freshly squeezed lime juice

Ice cubes

★ Blend the strawberries, sugar, and lime juice with 4 cups of water until very smooth. Strain the mixture through a sieve and into a large pitcher. Use a spoon to scoop off the foam that forms on the surface and discard it. Gradually season the agua fresca to taste with sugar and lime juice.

★ Chill the pitcher in the fridge, then stir thoroughly and pour the agua fresca into ice-filled glasses.

→ **MAKES 6 TO 8 TALL, ICY GLASSES**

MANGO-APPLE AGUA FRESCA

Agua de mango y manzana

Another great if unconventional agua. The combination of mango and apple produces a wonderful flavor, tropical and aromatic at first sip with a crisp, sweet finish.

~~~

1 large (about 1 pound) ripe mango, peeled, pitted, and cut into chunks

¼ cup sugar

¼ cup freshly squeezed lime juice

1 sweet apple, like Gala or Golden Delicious, quartered and cored

Ice cubes

★ Blend the mango, sugar, lime juice, and three-quarters of the apple with 4 cups of water until very smooth. Strain the mixture through a sieve and into a large pitcher. Gradually season the agua fresca to taste with more sugar and lime juice.

★ Chill the pitcher in the fridge, then stir thoroughly and pour the agua fresca into ice-filled glasses.

→ **MAKES 6 TO 8 TALL, ICY GLASSES**

PEANUT LIMEADE

Limonada de cacahuate

My American friends look at me funny when I talk up this concoction, my ode to two ingredients beloved by Mexicans. But for those of us born in a land where drinks are often made from flours, seeds, and nuts, the combination makes fine sense. Give it a chance and you'll be shocked at how lovely it is, the aroma and sweetness of peanuts giving way to a bolt of tart lime with each refreshing sip. Still feeling apprehensive? Add an ounce or so of rum to each glass.

~~~~~~~~~~~~~~~~

2 juicy limes, rinsed well, quartered, and seeds flicked out

½ cup unsalted roasted peanuts

⅓ cup sugar

Ice cubes

★ Blend the limes (yes, skin and all!), peanuts, and sugar with 2 cups of water until fairly smooth, at least 1 minute.

★ Strain the mixture through a sieve and into a medium pitcher, pressing on the solids to extract as much liquid as you can and discarding the solids. Add 1 cup of water and stir well, then pour the drink into ice-filled glasses and serve immediately.

→ **MAKES 6 TALL, ICY GLASSES**

HORCHATA

Now that rice milk has become a common sight on supermarket shelves, I occasionally skip the soaking, blending, and straining traditionally used to make horchata and simply tweak the flavor of the ready-made product. Of course, the quality and flavor differ widely by brand, so make sure to look for those without vanilla flavoring or added sugar. Either way, be cautious as you sweeten it.

→ **NOTE:** *The agave syrup is far from traditional. If you want to go the real Mexican route, swap in ¼ to ½ cup sweetened condensed milk.*

~~~~~~~~~~~~~~~~

4 cups unsweetened rice milk (from a 32-ounce container)

¼ cup agave syrup

½ teaspoon ground Mexican cinnamon, plus extra for garnish

Ice cubes

★ Briefly blend the rice milk, agave syrup, and cinnamon. Then pour the mixture into a large pitcher and refrigerate the horchata until it is well chilled.

★ Stir thoroughly, then pour the horchata into ice-filled glasses. Sprinkle each with a pinch of cinnamon and serve immediately.

→ **MAKES 6 TALL, ICY GLASSES**

STRAWBERRY SMOOTHIE

STRAWBERRY SMOOTHIE

Licuado de fresa

Hearty but not at all heavy, strawberry licuados are one of my favorite treats when I need a boost before a morning of market shopping, ogling xoconostles and chayotes between sweet sips.

1 pound ripe strawberries, hulled and chilled

½ cup powdered sugar

2 teaspoons vanilla extract

3 cups whole milk

A few pinches of ground Mexican cinnamon for sprinkling

★ Blend the strawberries, sugar, vanilla extract, and 2 cups of the milk in a blender until very smooth, about 2 minutes. Stir in the remaining 1 cup of milk and season to taste with sugar.

★ Pour the mixture into glasses, sprinkle a pinch of cinnamon over each one, and serve immediately.

→ **MAKES 4 GENEROUS PORTIONS**

BANANA SMOOTHIE

Licuado de plátano

As fantastic for breakfast as it is for dessert, this licuado isn't super thick and sugary, like a milk shake. Instead it's refreshing and filling with just a touch of sweetness. I love to drink it when it's especially cold, so be sure to chill the finished drink in the fridge.

3 large ripe bananas, peeled

2 cups whole milk

1 generous teaspoon vanilla extract

1 tablespoon sugar

¼ generous teaspoon ground Mexican cinnamon, plus ¼ teaspoon for sprinkling

★ Blend all the ingredients until very smooth, about 45 seconds. Chill briefly in the fridge, then pour the mixture into glasses, sprinkle a pinch of cinnamon over each one, and serve immediately.

→ **MAKES 2 LARGE OR 4 SMALLER DRINKS**

ORANGE, CARROT, AND PAPAYA SMOOTHIE WITH OATMEAL

Licuado de naranja, zanahoria, y papaya con avena

Every day before high school my friend Michele and I would gather around the blender to make a strange drink—milk and cocoa powder whizzed with corn flakes. Now that I'm older and, I like to think, a bit wiser, I start my mornings with a healthier smoothie that's made hearty with a different American breakfast staple, which in Mexico you're more likely to find in a cool drink like this than steaming hot in a bowl.

1 cup orange juice, preferably freshly squeezed, chilled

½ cup carrot juice, chilled

1 cup ripe papaya chunks, chilled

3 tablespoons quick-cooking rolled oats

1 tablespoon honey

1 tablespoon freshly squeezed lime juice

★ Combine all the ingredients in a blender and blend until smooth. Pour the mixture into a tall glass and drink immediately.

→ **MAKES 1 TALL GLASS**

THICK MEXICAN HOT CHOCOLATE
Champurrado de chocolate

Essentially an atole made with milk, the *champurrado* is a fantastic vehicle for chocolate. Because the drink is made thick with masa, not heavy cream, the result is comforting and satisfying but not heavy. I like mine slightly less sweet than those you'll typically find at the markets in Mexico, so if you have a sweeter tooth than I do, feel free to bump up the sugar to ⅓ cup.

⅓ cup tortilla flour (masa harina)

2 cups whole milk

6 ounces (about 2 disks) Mexican chocolate

¼ cup tightly-packed dark brown sugar

1 (4-inch) stick Mexican cinnamon

★ Blend the tortilla flour with 2½ cups of water until well combined, about 15 seconds. Pour the mixture into a medium pot, then add 2 more cups of water and the milk, chocolate, sugar, and cinnamon.

★ Set the pot over medium-high heat and bring the mixture to a simmer, stirring frequently to make sure the sugar doesn't stick to the bottom of the pot. Adjust the heat and simmer gently for 10 minutes, so the chocolate melts, the cinnamon steeps, and the flavors meld. If you'd like, gradually add more sugar to taste and simmer very gently for 2 to 3 minutes more. If the drink has lumps, strain the mixture through a sieve.

★ Ladle the hot atole into mugs, or cover and keep the drink warm over very low heat, gradually adding water to maintain the consistency.

→ **MAKES 6 TO 8 DRINKS**

PINEAPPLE ATOLE

Atole de piña

With its mellow sweetness and compulsive tang, this beverage will satisfy die-hard atole fans and, I hope, win many new ones. The lime juice is necessary only if your pineapple isn't tart enough.

½ cup tortilla flour (masa harina)

3 cups chopped ripe pineapple (about ½ pineapple)

½ cup tightly packed dark brown sugar or grated piloncillo

1 generous tablespoon crumbled Mexican cinnamon

⅛ teaspoon kosher salt

About 1 tablespoon freshly squeezed lime juice, if necessary

★ Pour 6 cups of water into a medium pot, then whisk in the tortilla flour. Blend the chopped pineapple in a blender until smooth and add it to the pot along with the sugar and cinnamon.

★ Set the pot over medium-high heat and bring the mixture to a simmer. Adjust the heat to maintain a gentle simmer and cook, skimming off any foam that develops on the surface, until the mixture thickens slightly, about 5 minutes.

★ Season the atole to taste with sugar and lime juice, bringing the liquid back to a simmer if you do. Strain the mixture into a separate pot, pressing on the solids to extract as much liquid as possible.

★ Ladle the hot atole into mugs, or cover and keep the drink warm over very low heat, gradually adding water to maintain the consistency.

→ SERVES 8

STRAWBERRY ATOLE
Atole de fresa

Atoles don't typically contain milk (which technically takes them into *champurrado* territory), yet this luxurious version does, a rich but far from heavy beverage alive with the flavor of fresh fruit. Look for strawberries that are ripe and red all the way through. If you can't find them, cook yours a bit longer than the twelve minutes I call for and consider adding a little more sugar.

1 pound fresh strawberries, hulled and
    roughly chopped

¾ cup sugar

1 (5-inch) piece Mexican cinnamon, crumbled

½ cup tortilla flour (masa harina)

¼ teaspoon kosher salt

4 cups whole milk

★ Combine the strawberries, sugar, and cinnamon in a medium pot, set the pot over medium heat, and cook, stirring occasionally, until the strawberries are completely soft, 10 to 12 minutes. The strawberries will be floating in bright-red liquid.

★ Meanwhile, blend the tortilla flour and salt with 2 cups of water until well combined, about 15 seconds. Combine the tortilla flour mixture and milk in a large pot, swishing some of the milk in the blender jar to loosen the remaining mixture and pouring that into the large pot, too. Set the pot over medium-high heat, stirring and scraping the bottom often, until the mixture comes to a vigorous simmer.

★ Reduce the heat to low. Rinse the blender and blend the strawberry mixture until fairly smooth, about 10 seconds. Strain the strawberry mixture into the milk mixture through a sieve, pressing on the solids to extract as much liquid as possible; discard the solids. Stir well. Swish 1 cup of the mixture into the blender and strain it into the strawberry mixture. Season to taste with sugar. Bring the mixture back to a simmer, then strain it once more.

★ Ladle the hot atole into mugs, or cover and keep the drink warm over very low heat, gradually adding water to maintain the consistency.

→ **SERVES 8 TO 10**

TAMARIND ATOLE

Atole de tamarindo

The tamarind-flavored version is a gateway atole: Try the warm, tangy drink once and you'll be eager to sample its siblings as well.

6 ounces tamarind pulp with seeds (slightly less than half a 14-ounce package)

1½ cups sugar

2 (5-inch) pieces Mexican cinnamon, crumbled

½ cup amaranth flour

★ Combine the tamarind, sugar, and 6 cups of water in a medium pot. Use your hands to break up the tamarind, set the pot over high heat, and bring the mixture to a boil. Add the cinnamon, then reduce the heat to maintain a steady simmer, and cook for 5 minutes.

★ Pour 4 cups of water into a medium bowl, add the amaranth flour, and stir well. Pour the flour mixture in a slow, steady stream into the tamarind mixture, whisking constantly. Let the mixture return to a simmer, then cook for 5 minutes, skimming off any foam that appears on the surface.

★ Season with sugar to taste and bring the liquid back to a simmer. Strain through a sieve into a separate pot, pressing on the solids to extract as much liquid as possible.

★ Ladle the hot atole into mugs, or cover and keep the drink warm over very low heat, gradually adding water to maintain the consistency.

→ **SERVES 8 TO 10**

MICHELADA

Save the fancy beers for another occasion. Micheladas are best with light, mild-flavored brews.

Generous 2 tablespoons freshly squeezed lime juice

Kosher salt

Ice cubes

2 firm shakes Worcestershire sauce

2 firm shakes hot sauce, such as Buffalo, Tabasco, or Valentina

1 (12-ounce) bottle or can Mexican beer, such as Corona, Sol, Pacifico, or Victoria

★ Moisten the rim of a tall glass with a little lime juice. Pour a generous amount of salt onto a small plate, invert the glass onto the salt, and rotate the glass to coat the rim with salt.

★ Fill the glass with the ice and add the remaining lime juice, the Worcestershire sauce, and the hot sauce. Serve with the beer alongside, pouring some into the glass and topping off your drink with more beer, as desired.

→ **MAKES 1 TALL, ICY GLASS**

CUCUMBER-GINGER MARGARITA

Margarita de pepino y jengibre

1¼ cups silver tequila

1 cup Cointreau

⅓ cup freshly squeezed lime juice
   (from about 3 juicy limes)

1 English cucumber, peeled and chopped

½ cup plus 2 tablespoons powdered sugar

2 teaspoons finely chopped peeled ginger

¼ teaspoon kosher salt

Ice cubes

★ Blend the tequila, Cointreau, lime juice, cucumber, sugar, ginger, and salt until smooth, about 45 seconds. Season to taste with lime juice and sugar. Strain the mixture through a sieve and into a pitcher, and refrigerate until cold.

★ Stir well, pour the mixture into 6 ice-filled glasses, and serve immediately.

→ MAKES 6 DRINKS

HIBISCUS MARGARITA

Margarita de jamaica

FOR THE SYRUP:

1 cup dried hibiscus flowers (jamaica)

½ cup sugar

FOR THE MARGARITAS:

1 cup plus 2 tablespoons silver tequila

Scant ½ cup Cointreau

Scant ½ cup freshly squeezed lime juice

Hibiscus Syrup (see above)

Ice cubes

TO MAKE THE SYRUP:

★ Rinse the flowers under running water.

★ Bring 2 cups of water to a boil in a small pot or saucepan. Add the hibiscus flowers and sugar, lower the heat to medium, and simmer steadily until the sugar dissolves and the syrup has thickened slightly, about 5 minutes. Strain the mixture through a sieve, discarding the solids, and let it cool. It makes about 1½ cups of syrup and keeps up to a week in the fridge.

TO MAKE THE MARGARITAS:

★ Combine the tequila, Cointreau, lime juice, all of the syrup, and 2 cups of ice in a pitcher and stir very well, at least 1 minute. It's important to stir for a full minute so some of the ice dissolves.

★ Pour the mixture into 6 ice-filled glasses and serve immediately.

→ MAKES 6 DRINKS

➔ **SALTING THE RIM:** *I love margaritas rimmed with salt, which brings out the saline notes in tequila, or Tajín brand chile seasoning, which you can pick up at nearly any Mexican market.*

1. *Squeeze enough lime juice onto a small plate to give you ⅛ inch or so and scatter a similar layer of kosher salt or chile seasoning on another.*

2. *One by one, turn the glasses so the outside of the rim is wet with lime juice, then place in the salt, turning each glass to ensure an even coating.*

HIBISCUS MARGARITA

PINEAPPLE MARGARITA

Margarita de piña

2 cups (¾-inch chunks) peeled ripe pineapple

1 cup silver tequila

¼ cup plus 2 tablespoons Cointreau

½ cup plus 2 tablespoons freshly squeezed
lime juice (from about 5 juicy limes)

¼ cup sugar

10 spearmint leaves

Ice cubes

★ Blend the pineapple, tequila, Cointreau, lime juice, and sugar until smooth, about 45 seconds. Season to taste with lime juice and sugar. Add the mint and blend briefly so the mixture is flecked with green. Pour the mixture into a pitcher and refrigerate until cold.

★ Stir well, pour the mixture into 6 ice-filled glasses, and serve immediately.

⇢ **MAKES 6 DRINKS**

ROBIN'S WATER-MELON PUNCH

Jarro de sandia

2 fresh spearmint sprigs

4 cups watermelon juice (8 cups cubed, ripe
watermelon, seeded, blended, and strained)

2 cups vodka

1 cup ginger liqueur, such as
Domaine de Canton

½ cup freshly squeezed lime juice (from about
4 juicy limes)

Ice cubes

★ Muddle the mint in a large pitcher.

★ Add the watermelon juice, vodka, ginger liqueur, and lime juice to the pitcher, stir well, and refrigerate for up to 4 hours.

★ Stir well, pour the mixture into 8 ice-filled glasses, and serve immediately.

⇢ **MAKES 8 DRINKS**

PINEAPPLE MARGARITA

MANGO TORITO
Torito de mango

PEANUT TORITO
Torito de cacahuate

Traditionally made from *agua ardiente*, toritos work well with other sugarcane spirits, like rum, cachaça, and pisco. Keep in mind that the sweetness and strength of each drink is ultimately up to you.

〰〰〰〰〰〰〰〰〰〰〰

1 large (about 1 pound) ripe mango or 1 cup mango puree, thawed if frozen

1 cup rum, cachaça, or pisco

1 cup superfine sugar

½ cup freshly squeezed lime juice

Ice cubes

★ If using fresh mango, cut the flesh through the skin on both sides of the pit. Cut the flesh in a cross-hatched pattern (avoid piercing the skin) and use a spoon to scoop the flesh into the blender. Trim off the flesh still clinging to the pit and add it to the blender. Blend until smooth. Measure out 1 cup of the puree, reserving the rest for another purpose.

★ Combine the 1 cup of mango puree, rum, sugar, and lime juice with 2 cups of water in a pitcher. Stir until the sugar has completely dissolved.

★ Pour the mixture into 6 ice-filled glasses and serve immediately.

→ **MAKES 6 DRINKS**

½ cup smooth peanut butter (well stirred, if necessary)

¼ cup sugar

1 teaspoon ground Mexican cinnamon

Pinch of salt (if using unsalted peanut butter)

¾ cup rum, cachaça, or pisco

8 wide strips lime zest

Ice cubes

★ Combine the peanut butter, sugar, cinnamon, salt, and 3 cups of water in a blender jar. Blend until smooth, at least 30 seconds to be sure the sugar fully dissolves. Pour the mixture into a large pitcher and stir in the rum.

★ Bend or twist the lime strips over 8 ice-filled glasses, then drop the lime strips into the glasses. Pour the torito into the glasses and serve immediately.

→ **MAKES 8 DRINKS**

PEANUT TORITO

★ ★ ★

DESSERTS

FOR A SWEET ENDING TO A SAVORY BOOK, I've channeled the simplicity of tacos and tortas to create recipes for astoundingly easy-to-make desserts, including some of the tastiest everyday sweets of Mexico. That means stir-and-bake cakes and blend-and-serve custards; piecrust that doesn't require a moment of kneading, let alone a stand mixer; and frozen treats that are ready for the ice cream machine in no time.

CHOCOLATE PUDDING
Pudín de chocolate

☆ ☆ ☆ ☆ ☆ △ △ ☆

These individual silky confections are my ode to the versions I remember eagerly grabbing from supermarket shelves and piling into my mom's shopping cart. The flavor and texture of homemade pudding, of course, are superior in every way, particularly when the pudding is served alongside a little candied orange rind, or topped with a dollop of whipped cream and perhaps crumbled sugared pecans.

★ Combine the milk and cream in a medium pot, and set the pot over medium-high heat. Split the vanilla bean lengthwise, scrape in the seeds, and drop in the pod. Stir in the sugar, cinnamon, espresso powder, and salt. Cook, stirring, until the sugar has dissolved completely. Add the chocolate and cook, whisking frequently, until it's fully melted and you have a very smooth brown liquid, 3 to 4 minutes.

★ Transfer the mixture to a bowl and let it cool completely, stirring frequently to prevent a skin from forming on the surface. To chill it quickly, set the bowl in a larger bowl filled with ice water, stirring occasionally.

★ Preheat the oven to 300°F. Bring about 8 cups of water to a boil in a kettle or pot. Once the pudding mixture is cool, whisk in the egg yolks until well blended, then strain the mixture through a sieve, discarding the solids.

★ Arrange the ramekins in a large baking dish, roasting pan, or skillet. Carefully fill each ramekin with the pudding mixture, stopping about ½ inch short of the brim. Very carefully pour enough boiling water into the large dish to come halfway up the sides of the ramekins.

★ Bake just until the edges have set but the center still wobbles when you gently shake the pan, 30 to 45 minutes. Let the pudding come to room temperature and serve or refrigerate for up to three days and serve chilled.

3 cups whole milk

1 cup heavy cream

1 vanilla bean, or 2 teaspoons vanilla extract

⅔ cup sugar

2 teaspoons ground Mexican cinnamon

Scant ½ teaspoon instant espresso powder (optional)

1 teaspoon kosher salt

9 ounces chopped bittersweet chocolate (about 2 cups)

10 large egg yolks

EQUIPMENT:
Twelve 4-ounce ramekins

→ **SERVES 12** ★

LIME PIE
Pay de limón

FOR THE CRUST:

2½ ounces Maria brand cookies or graham
    crackers, coarsely crumbled

⅔ cup pecans

2 teaspoons sugar

½ teaspoon ground Mexican cinnamon

¼ teaspoon kosher salt

3 tablespoons unsalted butter, melted

FOR THE FILLING:

8 large egg yolks

2 (14-ounce) cans sweetened condensed milk

2 lightly packed tablespoons finely grated
    lime zest (from about 2 limes)

1¼ cups freshly squeezed lime juice,
    (from about 10 juicy limes) strained

Generous 1 teaspoon vanilla extract

1¼ teaspoons kosher salt

EQUIPMENT:

9-inch pie dish (even a disposable foil one)

→ **SERVES 8** ★

The pie is one of the many culinary imports to Mexico taken up enthusiastically by its citizens. Today, kids clamor for little packaged pineapple pies and pecan pies. We've even adopted the word—spelled "pay" in phonetic Spanish. And as you might expect, when we discovered that one could make pie from our favorite fruit, the lime, that particular pie became a dessert staple. This version couldn't be easier: a simple crust made from crushed cookies that requires no kneading and a filling that requires only a bowl, a whisk, and two minutes of your time.

The pie is excellent without embellishment, but I like to top slices with dollops of whipped cream and a grating of lime zest.

MAKE THE CRUST:

★ Position the rack in the center and preheat the oven to 350°F.

★ Stir together the cookies, pecans, sugar, cinnamon, and salt in a mixing bowl. Add the mixture to a small food processor and grind, in batches, if necessary, just until you have a mixture of coarse and fine crumbs (some the size of lentils, some like grains of sand). Transfer them to a bowl.

★ Add the melted butter to the crumb mixture, a tablespoon or two at a time, stirring between each addition to evenly moisten the crumbs. You'll have a rather loose, crumbly mixture.

★ Use your fingers to pack the mixture in an even layer against the bottom and nearly all the way up the sides of the pie pan. Bake just until the crust is fragrant and golden brown, just a shade or two darker than when it started, about 15 minutes. Let it cool completely.

★ **MAKE AHEAD:** The crust keeps covered in the fridge for up to two days or in the freezer for up to one month. Defrost the crust in the fridge before baking.

MAKE THE FILLING AND BAKE THE PIE:

★ Preheat the oven to 350°F. Briefly whisk the yolks in a large bowl, then add the condensed milk, lime zest and juice, vanilla extract, and salt. Whisk until very well blended, then carefully pour the mixture into the cooled piecrust.

★ Bake the pie just until the edges of the filling are set but the center still wobbles slightly when you gently shake the pan, 20 to 25 minutes. Let it come to room temperature and serve or refrigerate for up to two days and serve chilled.

MANGO CREAM WITH BERRIES

Crema de mango con moras

This recipe is for lazy cooks, as sometimes we all can be. An arrow in the quiver of so many Mexican cooks, it relies on a bit of culinary magic to replicate the rich texture of old-fashioned custard desserts. You toss all the ingredients in the blender and whiz for a few minutes until the culinary alchemy reveals itself: the acidity of the mangoes and lime thickens the milks and the orange-hued cream sets almost like custard. Once it does, top it with berries or serve it alongside cookies or wafers. Occasionally, I'll gussy up these combinations, creating pretty layers of cream, crumbled cookies or granola, and bananas or berries in glass jars.

★ Combine the mangoes, the milks, and lime juice in a blender and blend on high for 30 seconds, then taste and add more lime juice, if necessary. Continue blending for 2½ minutes more, so the cream can properly thicken.

★ Transfer the mango cream to a large container, cover with plastic wrap, and refrigerate for at least 4 hours or up to 24 hours. It will thicken further.

★ Halve or quarter any large berries. Layer the mango cream with the berries or compote in serving bowls or glasses. Serve right away.

1½ pounds ripe mangoes (about 2 large), peeled and pitted

1 (14-ounce) can sweetened condensed milk

1 (12-ounce) can evaporated milk, shaken

Generous 3 tablespoons freshly squeezed lime juice, or more to taste

3 cups mixed fresh berries or Berry Compote (page 220)

→ SERVES 10 TO 12 ★

COCONUT RICE PUDDING
Arroz con coco

☆ ☆

1 cup uncooked long-grain white rice

1 (6-inch) stick Mexican cinnamon, preferably tied with butcher's twine if flaky

½ cup unsweetened shredded coconut

6 cups whole milk

1 cup heavy cream

¼ teaspoon kosher salt

1 cup sugar

Finely grated zest of 1 small lime (about 1 tablespoon)

½ to ¾ cup raisins (optional)

→ **SERVES 8** ★

In Mexico, even sweets are hawked from the streets. Vendors amble through squares carrying glass boxes filled with a colorful array of gelatins, flans, and puddings, like this one, individually wrapped and fastened with rubber bands. Rice pudding is popular in home kitchens too, a one-pot dessert that feeds many with little effort.

The flavor of Mexican cinnamon is a must, though if you can't find it, you can mimic its flavor here with two sticks of regular cinnamon and a vanilla bean. In fact, the versions I've shared at the homes of friends in Mexico are often flavored with so much of the spice that every mouthful of pudding brings with it a few tough bits of cinnamon bark. I use plenty myself, stirring carefully or even tying the cinnamon stick with butcher's twine to spare you those bits. I also love the extra layers of flavor and aroma provided by coconut and lime zest. Mexican cooks put raisins in just about every dessert imaginable. Here, they're optional.

★ Put the rice and cinnamon in a medium pot and add 3 cups of water. Bring the water to a boil over high heat, then lower the heat to cook at a steady simmer, stirring occasionally, until the water has almost completely evaporated but the rice is still quite firm, about 10 minutes.

★ Raise the heat again, then add the milk, cream, and salt, and bring to a boil. Lower the heat to maintain a gentle boil and cook, stirring occasionally to prevent the rice from sticking to the bottom of the pot and the liquids from boiling over, until the rice is tender and the mixture is slightly thickened (it will thicken significantly after it cools), 15 to 20 minutes. Stir in the sugar, return the mixture to a simmer, and cook for just a minute or so more. Stir in the lime zest and raisins, if using them.

★ Transfer the pudding to a container, let it cool slightly, then discard the cinnamon. Press a sheet of plastic wrap directly onto the surface of the pudding to prevent a skin from forming. Refrigerate the pudding until it's cold, at least 1 hour or up to three days.

CAJETA-BANANA BREAD PUDDING
Budín de pan con plátano y cajeta

☆☆☆☆☆☆☆☆☆☆☆☆☆☆☆☆☆☆△△△△△△△△△△☆☆☆☆☆☆☆☆☆☆☆☆

Bread pudding is a staple in many nations of frugal and ingenious cooks. Whenever my family found itself with stale *bolillos*, my grandmother soaked them in milk, eggs, butter, and sugar and baked them to create a dense pudding—studded with raisins, because she added raisins to everything. Nowadays, I prefer an airier, fluffier version made with breads like challah or brioche, served warm with ice cream, homemade (page 200) or store-bought, melting on top.

★ Preheat the oven to 350°F.

★ Spread the bread in one layer on a baking sheet and cook in the oven until the cubes feel dry on the outside but not colored, about 15 minutes. Let them cool. Leave the oven on.

★ Meanwhile, combine the milk, cajeta, cinnamon, vanilla extract, and salt in a medium saucepan. Set the pan over medium heat and stir often until the cajeta is completely melted. Take the pan off the heat, whisk in the cream, then whisk in the eggs.

★ Put the bread and bananas in a large bowl. Pour in half of the cajeta mixture, toss well, and let the bread sit for 15 minutes to soak up the liquid. Add the rest of the cajeta mixture, toss, and let it all sit for another 15 minutes.

★ Toss the mixture once more and put it into the buttered dish in an even layer. It's fine if the bread towers over the rim. Bake until the top is slightly crunchy and browned at the edges and a knife inserted into the center comes out moist but clean, 30 to 35 minutes. Let the bread pudding cool slightly before you eat it.

1 (1-pound) brioche or challah loaf, crusts removed, cut into ½-inch chunks (generous 8 cups of chunks)

1 cup whole milk

1 cup cajeta

1 teaspoon ground Mexican cinnamon

1 teaspoon vanilla extract

⅛ teaspoon kosher salt

1½ cups heavy cream

3 large eggs

2 bananas, peeled and thinly sliced

EQUIPMENT:
One 1½- to 2-quart shallow pie dish or baking dish, buttered

→ **SERVES 8** ★

DATE-PECAN CAKE
Pastelito de dátil y nuez

☆ ☆

Generous 1 cup pecan halves (about 5 ounces)

4 tablespoons unsalted butter, at room temperature, plus more for coating the pan

2 tablespoons sugar

1 pound pitted dates, roughly chopped

Generous 1 tablespoon vanilla extract

1 teaspoon baking soda

2 large eggs

1½ cups lightly packed dark brown sugar

Finely grated zest of 1 orange (about 1 tablespoon)

1 teaspoon baking powder

2 teaspoons kosher salt

½ cup chopped semisweet chocolate or chocolate chips (optional)

2 cups all-purpose flour

EQUIPMENT:
10-inch square baking pan

→ **SERVES 12** ★

I can't get enough of this sticky, moist cake—the texture not unlike that of England's steamed pudding—with the complex sweetness of dates balanced with the brightness of orange zest. Best of all, the cake is exceedingly simple. No stand mixer and no beating required! I love the addition of chocolate and a finishing drizzle of Mexican crema, but those embellishments are up to you.

★ Preheat the oven to 350°F. Spread the pecans in one layer on a baking sheet and bake, shaking and tossing once or twice, until they're very fragrant and a shade or two darker, about 5 minutes. Set them aside to cool.

★ Butter the cake pan, then add the sugar and rotate the pan to coat it with the sugar, then dump out any excess.

★ Combine the dates, vanilla extract, and 1½ cups of water in a medium pot and set the pot over high heat. Once the liquid comes to a boil, turn off the heat, add the baking soda, and stir well. It'll fizz and bubble. Transfer the mixture to a large bowl and let cool to room temperature.

★ Stir in the butter and mix until well blended, then add the eggs, brown sugar, orange zest, baking powder, salt, toasted pecans, and chocolate, mixing well after each addition. Sift in the flour and stir really well to blend.

★ Pour the batter into the prepared cake pan, firmly shake the pan back and forth and side to side, then firmly knock the bottom against the counter once or twice. This ensures the batter is evenly distributed in the pan and that there are no bubbles.

★ Bake the cake until a toothpick or skewer stuck into the center comes out moist but clean, about 45 minutes.

★ Let the cake cool to room temperature. Invert the cake onto a plate (you'll have to give the pan a firm shake and might have to slide a knife around the edge of the cake to loosen it) and turn the cake right side up.

★ **MAKE AHEAD:** The cake keeps in the fridge for up to three days.

→ AN ADULT TWIST: *For an even more moist and lovely cake, I drizzle this simple tequila syrup over it, just a teaspoon over each side of each slice or half of the syrup over the whole cake before slicing it.*

Combine ½ CUP SUGAR and ½ CUP WATER in a small saucepan. Bring to a boil *over medium-high heat, stirring until the sugar dissolves completely. Add ¼ CUP WHITE TEQUILA, return the mixture to a boil, and remove the pan from the heat.*

If you'd like, add a couple strips of orange peel or a three-inch piece of Mexican cinnamon to the pot with the sugar and water.

FLAN

FOR THE FLAN:

1 (14-ounce) can sweetened
   condensed milk

1½ cups whole milk

¼ cup sugar

2 heaping tablespoons
   coarsely crumbled
   Mexican cinnamon

Zest of ½ lime, removed in
   thick strips, white pith
   scraped off

Zest of 1 small lemon,
   removed in thick strips,
   white pith scraped off

¼ teaspoon kosher salt

4 large eggs

4 large egg yolks

FOR THE CARAMEL:

½ cup sugar

Generous 1 teaspoon freshly
   squeezed lime juice

⅛ teaspoon kosher salt

EQUIPMENT:

9-inch round shallow (about
   1½-inch deep) cake pan

→ SERVES 8 ★

The Spanish-style custard has been so enthusiastically adopted by Mexicans that now every one of my friends insists that his grandmother makes the best flan. Me, I adore any version that's velvety but not too rich or sweet. I love the way the solid caramel layer that lines your pan melts into a syrup that coats the flan, adding a hint of bitterness to counter the lavishly creamy custard, which I infuse with the subtle flavors of cinnamon and citrus zest.

➤ **TIP:** *As soon as you've coated the baking dish with the caramel, fill the pot in which you made the caramel with water. This will save you a lot of scrubbing and grief later on.*

PREPARE THE FLAN:

★ Combine the condensed milk, whole milk, sugar, cinnamon, lime and lemon zests, and salt in a medium saucepan and bring the mixture to a boil over medium-high heat, stirring frequently, and immediately take the pan off the heat.

★ Whisk the eggs and yolks together in a large bowl to blend. Pour the milk mixture into the bowl in a slow, steady stream, whisking constantly. Cover and let the mixture steep for at least 30 minutes.

★ MAKE AHEAD: If you'd like, press a sheet of plastic wrap directly onto the surface of the flan mixture to prevent a skin from forming and refrigerate for up to two days. Bring the mixture to room temperature and stir well before proceeding.

☆ ☆

MAKE THE CARAMEL:

★ Preheat the oven to 325°F.

★ Heat the sugar, lime juice, and salt with 2 tablespoons of water in a small saucepan over medium-high heat. Stir until the mixture begins to simmer, then bring to a rapid boil. Cook, without stirring, until the mixture turns a light brown color, about 2½ minutes. Keep a close eye on the mixture, gently swirling the liquid occasionally to get a better sense of its color below the bubbles, until it turns a deep brown color, about 2 minutes more.

★ Immediately pour the mixture into the cake pan and quickly rotate the pan so the caramel evenly coats the bottom and about halfway up the sides.

BAKE THE FLAN:

★ Bring about 8 cups of water to a boil in a kettle or pot. Strain the flan mixture through a sieve into the caramel-lined cake pan.

★ Carefully place the cake pan in a baking pan, roasting pan, or skillet that's large enough to the fit the cake pan comfortably. Set it on the oven rack. Carefully pour enough boiling water into the larger pan to come halfway up the sides of the cake pan. Bake just until the edges are set but the center still wobbles when you gently shake the pan, 45 minutes to 1 hour.

★ Let it cool in the water, then remove the cake pan from the water. Cover with plastic wrap and refrigerate for at least 8 hours or up to two days.

★ Run the tip of a small knife around the edge of the flan, give the pan a gentle shake, then carefully invert the flan onto a plate. Eat cold or at room temperature.

BAKED PLANTAINS
Plátanos asados

☆ ☆

A long, low whistle signals the arrival of the *camotero*, a vendor who pushes his old-fashioned cart, with its signature smokestack and wood fire that burns beneath. He sells *camotes* (sweet potatoes) and plantains, both slowly roasted until they're soft and sugary. A drizzle of sweetened condensed milk makes these an especially rich street snack. Every so often, the vendor releases steam, producing that familiar whistle, an announcement to anyone in the square or houses nearby that the *camotero* has arrived.

4 large very ripe (peels almost completely black) plantains

A few tablespoons sweetened condensed milk

→ **SERVES 4** ★

★ Preheat the oven to 350°F.

★ Put the plantains, unpeeled, on a foil-lined baking sheet and cook them in the oven for 30 minutes. Use a small knife to remove half the peel so one side of each plantain is exposed and the other is cradled in peel. Cook in the oven, peel sides down, until the fruit is very soft, about 15 minutes more.

★ Transfer the plantains, peel and all, to plates and drizzle sweetened condensed milk over each one. Serve while they're still hot.

MASHED SWEET POTATO with PINEAPPLE
Puré de camote con piña

☆ ☆

3½ pounds sweet potatoes

1 stick unsalted butter, cut into ½-inch pieces

½ cup honey, or more to taste

2 tablespoons freshly squeezed lime juice

2 teaspoons kosher salt

1 ½ teaspoons árbol chile powder (optional), or more to taste

3 cups (½-inch cubes) pineapple (from about ½ fresh pineapple)

··················
→ **SERVES 6** ★
··················

Although I'd happily set out this sweet, tart, spicy dish as a side, I love serving it as dessert, perhaps topped with a melting blob of lightly sweetened whipped cream.

~~~~~~~~

★ Preheat the oven to 400°F. Poke each sweet potato in several places with a knife and arrange them on a foil-lined baking sheet. Bake until the potatoes are soft all the way through, 40 minutes to 1 hour, depending on the size of the potatoes.

★ Use tongs to remove the peel. Transfer the sweet potato flesh to a medium pot or serving bowl and mash it coarsely. While it's still warm, stir the butter, honey, lime juice, salt, and árbol chile powder, if using it. Fold in the pineapple.

★ Season to taste with more honey, árbol chile powder, and salt.

BERRY COMPOTE
Compota de moras

☆ ☆

½ pint fresh blackberries, halved if large

½ pint fresh blueberries

½ pint fresh raspberries

½ cup powdered sugar

2 tablespoons freshly squeezed lime juice

1 (4-inch) piece Mexican cinnamon

⅛ teaspoon kosher salt

....
→ **MAKES 2
GENEROUS CUPS ★**
....

Sweet and tart with lots of berry flavor, this compote makes a fine accompaniment for Flan (page 192), but is equally appealing with pound cake, pancakes, ice cream, or even layered with Mango Cream with Berries (page 187).

★ Combine all the ingredients in a medium saucepan, stir well, and set the pan over medium-high heat.

★ Soon the berries will begin to give up their juices. Bring the liquid to a boil, then lower the heat to maintain a steady simmer. Cook, stirring gently so you don't break up the berries too much, until the liquid in the compote reaches the level of the berries and many of the berries are still intact, about 3 minutes.

★ Discard the cinnamon. Let the compote cool to room temperature (it will thicken) before using for the flan.

★ **MAKE AHEAD:** The compote keeps, covered, in the fridge for up to two days.

MEXICAN CHOCOLATE ICE CREAM
Helado de chocolate mexicana

☆ ☆

The Mexican chocolate widely available in the U.S. works great in adobo, moles, and many desserts. Yet when I really want to highlight the flavor of the cinnamon-scented cocoa, I look to the artisanal stone-ground stuff that you might find in Oaxaca, but that you'd struggle to find in Omaha. No matter, you can easily ape the flavor with high-quality European or American chocolate mixed with Mexican cinnamon, as I do in this recipe. If you can get your hands on crunchy, chocolate-covered cocoa nibs, mix in a cup or so after processing in the ice cream maker for a fun take on that wonderful, very American flavor: chocolate chocolate chip.

1½ cups heavy cream

1½ cups whole milk

¼ pound bittersweet dark chocolate (preferably 62% cocao), broken into pieces

½ cup honey

Scant ½ cup crumbled Mexican cinnamon (about ¾ ounce)

¼ cup unsweetened cocoa powder

1 teaspoon vanilla extract

Generous ¼ teaspoon kosher salt

10 large egg yolks

→ **MAKES ABOUT 1½ QUARTS** ★

★ Combine the cream, milk, chocolate, honey, cinnamon, cocoa powder, vanilla extract, and salt in a medium pot. Bring the mixture to a simmer over medium-high heat, whisking often, and cook until the chocolate has melted completely, then continue cooking for 2 minutes more, to let the cinnamon steep.

★ In a large bowl, whisk the egg yolks until smooth, then use a ladle to gradually add about 1 cup of the hot milk mixture to the yolks, whisking vigorously and constantly. Pour the contents of the bowl into the pot, whisking until well incorporated.

★ Press a sheet of plastic wrap directly onto the surface of the custard to prevent a skin from forming and refrigerate the custard until it is cold or for up to one day. If you'd like to chill it quickly, set the bowl of custard in a larger bowl filled with ice water, stirring frequently, until it is well chilled.

★ Put the chilled custard into an ice cream maker and process according to the manufacturer's instructions, until it's firm enough to scoop. Eat the ice cream right away or divide it among airtight containers and freeze it for up to a month.

MEXICAN-STYLE FROZEN CUSTARD
Amantecado

☆ ☆

2 cups heavy cream

2 cups whole milk

1 vanilla bean, split lengthwise

¼ cup coarsely crumbled
Mexican cinnamon

3 wide strips orange zest
(about 3×1½ inches),
white pith scraped off

Zest of ½ lime, removed
in strips, white pith
scraped off

¾ cup sugar

8 large egg yolks

....
→ **MAKES ABOUT
2 QUARTS ★**
....

This recipe—my take on the custard-based ice cream called *amantecado*—is meant to serve as the base for Tequila-Raisin Ice Cream (opposite page). Yet it's so delicious already, infused with cinnamon and citrus, that you'll happily devour it plain. It's also great with hot fudge, Berry Compote (page 198), or Cajeta-Banana Bread Pudding (page 189), or even simply chilled (not churned in the ice cream maker) and spiked with rum—the eggnog-like result that's very similar to what Mexicans call *rompope*.

★ Combine the cream, milk, vanilla bean, cinnamon, and zests in a medium pot and bring the mixture to a boil over medium-high heat, stirring frequently to make sure the milk doesn't scorch.

★ Meanwhile, whisk the sugar and yolks together in a large bowl just until the sugar dissolves and the mixture thickens, about 45 seconds.

★ Pour the milk mixture in a slow, steady stream into the yolk mixture, whisking constantly. Then pour the bowl's contents back into the pot. Set the heat to medium-low and cook, constantly stirring and gently scraping the bottom with a wooden spoon or flexible spatula. Watch closely as the foam on the surface subsides and the bubbles become smaller. You're waiting for the moment that the foam disappears altogether, about 4 minutes after it has formed. The mixture will have thickened slightly, enough to just coat the back of a spoon. The second it does, remove the pan from the heat and strain the mixture through a sieve and into a clean bowl.

★ Press a sheet of plastic wrap directly onto the surface of the custard to prevent a skin from forming and refrigerate the custard until it is cold or for up to one day. If you'd like to chill it quickly, set the bowl of custard in a larger bowl filled with ice water, stirring frequently, until it is well chilled.

★ Put the chilled custard into an ice cream maker and process according to the manufacturer's instructions, until it's firm enough to scoop. Eat the ice cream right away or divide it among airtight containers and freeze it for up to a month.

TEQUILA-RAISIN ICE CREAM

☆ ☆ ☆ ☆ ☆ ☆ ☆ ☆ ☆ ☆ ☆ ☆ ☆ ☆ ☆ ☆ ☆ ☆ ★ ★ ☆ ☆ ☆ ☆ ☆ ☆ ☆ ☆ ☆ ☆ ☆ ☆ ☆ ☆ ☆ ☆ ☆

In the Mexican version of the classic American rum raisin ice cream, each creamy bite delivers raisins that have been steeped in tequila, plump and thrilling with the tickle of alcohol.

★ Heat tequila with ¼ cup of water in a small saucepan just until it simmers. Put the raisins in a small bowl, pour in the hot liquid, and let the raisins soak for at least 2 hours, or cover and refrigerate the mixture overnight.

★ Strain the raisins, discarding the liquid. Stir the raisins into the ice cream right after processing in the ice cream maker but before freezing.

➜ **TIP:** *To protect against those little cities of ice crystals cropping up on the surface of the ice cream, either pack the containers to the brim or press a circle of parchment paper against the surface before adding the cover.*

½ cup añejo tequila

1 cup raisins

1 cup Mexican-Style Frozen Custard (opposite page, processed but not frozen)

....

➜ **MAKES ABOUT 2 QUARTS ★**

....

PINEAPPLE-MINT SORBET

Nieves de piña y yerba buena

☆ ☆

½ cup sugar (or up to ¾ cup if your pineapple isn't very sweet)

4 cups fresh pineapple juice (from 1 peeled, blended, and strained ripe pineapple)

½ cup freshly squeezed lime juice (from about 4 juicy limes), or more to taste

1 generous teaspoon finely grated peeled ginger

¼ teaspoon kosher salt

2 tablespoons very finely chopped spearmint leaves

→ **MAKES ABOUT 6 CUPS** ★

While not so common in icy treats in Mexico, pineapple's partnership with mint gives the tart fruit a whole new dimension of flavor. You'll find yourself playing with the amounts of lime and sugar to account for pineapple that's less sweet or more acidic. This sorbet is best eaten within a few days, because the mint will begin to discolor.

★ Combine the sugar and 1½ cups of water in a medium saucepan. Bring the mixture to a full boil over medium-high heat, stirring, just until the sugar has dissolved completely. Transfer the mixture to a bowl and let it cool completely. (To chill it quickly, set the bowl in a larger bowl filled with ice water, stirring occasionally.)

★ Stir together the sugar mixture, pineapple juice, lime juice, ginger, and salt, and process the mixture in an ice cream maker according to the manufacturer's instructions, until it's firm enough to scoop. Add the mint and continue to process just until it's well distributed, about 2 minutes. Eat the sorbet right away or divide it among airtight containers and freeze it for up to a month.

LIME SORBET
Nieve de limón

The memory of the vivid green lime drinks sold streetside and in markets—made from whole limes (peel, pith, and all!)—inspired this sorbet. Instead of just juice, I use lots of lime zest to add aroma and color for an incredibly refreshing end to a meal. The greener the limes, the more striking the color of the final product.

1 cup sugar

2 tablespoons finely grated lime zest (from about 3 limes)

1½ cups freshly squeezed lime juice (from about 10 juicy limes)

¼ teaspoon kosher salt

→ **MAKES 1 QUART** ★

★ Combine the sugar and 2 cups of water in a medium saucepan. Bring the mixture to a full boil over medium-high heat, stirring, just until the sugar has dissolved completely. Transfer the mixture to a bowl and let it cool completely. (To chill it quickly, set the bowl in a larger bowl filled with ice water, stirring occasionally.)

★ Whisk together the sugar mixture with the lime juice, zest, and salt, and process in an ice cream maker according to the manufacturer's instructions, until it's firm enough to scoop. Eat the sorbet right away or divide it among airtight containers and freeze it for up to a month.

GLOSSARY

☆ ☆

AVOCADO: The Mexican Hass avocado, with its creamy flesh and full flavor, is the avocado of choice for this book and for the majority of Mexican dishes. I'm particularly fond of Hass avocados from Mexico, so look for the country of origin on the little sticker on the fruit's pebbly skin.

Avocados slowly ripen at room temperature, the flesh getting creamier and more delicious by the day. You may find avocados at the market that range from unripe (very firm) to overripe (mushy). Unripe avocados take several days to fully ripen. Avoid avocados that feel mushy, have any too-soft spots, or whose skin has separated from the flesh.

Store ripe avocados in the fridge for up to three days. Keep any leftover avocado in the fridge, with plastic wrap pressed tightly against the flesh to minimize browning, for a day or so. Let the fruit come to room temperature before you use it.

BANANA LEAVES: You'll find large, glossy leaves of the banana plant in Latin and Asian markets, often in the freezer section. Either defrost them in the fridge or, to do it more quickly, put the plastic bag of leaves under cold running water. Wipe the leaves on both sides with a damp paper towel and trim off any brown edges before using. If you are lucky enough to find a market that offers a selection, look for thin, pliable leaves.

CHEESE: Mexico has a rich cheese-making tradition and these three cheeses are worth seeking out. Of course, there are many delicious cheeses that work well as alternatives, so I've offered suggestions for them, too.

- **Chihuahua cheese:** A lovely mild cheese that gets perfectly gooey when melted. Monterrey jack, soft provolone, or even cheddar make solid substitutes.
- **Oaxaca cheese** (also called quesillo): Firm string cheese from Mexico via the Middle East. Try subbing Armenian string cheese without nigella seeds or mozzarella.
- **Queso fresco:** Salty and slightly crumbly. Feta or ricotta salata works well in its place, though they're both slightly saltier.

CHILES: The recipes in this book call for just a handful of the many chiles, fresh and dried, in the Mexican repertoire. To ensure accessible recipes, I have limited myself to the most readily available chiles in the U.S. They're available in Mexican and Latin supermarkets and by mail order. (See sources, page 210).

FRESH CHILES: Look for fresh chiles that are free of blemishes and wrinkles. Because fresh chiles of the same kind can vary widely in spiciness (I can't tell you how many jalapeños I've come across in the U.S. that have no heat at all!), always buy a few more than you'll need for a particular recipe so you can adjust the heat level.

Store fresh chiles in a plastic bag in the fridge for up to a week. Habanero chiles can be frozen and defrosted before use.

- **Poblano** – Mild (though some do provide a tingle) with a lovely sweet-bitter quality when roasted
- **Jalapeño** – Bright, sharp heat and green flavor

- **Serrano** – Like a jalapeño, but with a grassier flavor and sharper heat
- **Habanero** – Floral, aromatic, and fiercely spicy

DRIED CHILES: Look for dried chiles that are supple, not brittle; more or less unbroken; and have minimal pale spots.

Store dried chiles in an airtight resealable bag, and keep them in a cool, dry place for up to six months.

TRICK: Can only find brittle dried chiles? Try this: Put them in an airtight resealable bag with a square of just-damp paper towel and by the next day, they'll be supple.
- **Ancho** – Slightly spicy and fleshy with a prune-like sweetness
- **Árbol** – Fiery with a subtle acidity and nutty quality (*Note: Don't be fooled by chiles that are labeled "árbol" but bear little resemblance in flavor to the real thing. Look for longer, more cylindrical, less wrinkly chiles from Mexico, with at least some stems attached.*)
- **Guajillo** – Mild and fruity with a hint of citrus
- **Chipotle** – Smoky, spicy, and subtly sweet (*Note: There are two main varieties of chipotles available in the U.S. For the purposes of this book, look for chipotles moras, which are small and dark purple, rather than elongated, tobacco-colored chipotles mecos. The two are not interchangeable.*)

CHILE POWDER: Several recipes call for chipotle or árbol chile powder, which is easy to make, stays potent for up to three months in a cool, dark place, and provides an effortless way to add the character and heat of those chiles to your everyday meals. Chipotle powder is available in most supermarkets, but it's even better made at home.

....

1 ounce dried chipotle mora chiles (8 to 10, purplish-red color) or dried árbol chiles (30 to 40), wiped clean and stemmed

Heat a heavy skillet over medium-low heat (for chipotle chiles) or low heat (for árbol chiles).

Toast the chipotles, turning them over occasionally, until they blister in spots (some will puff up), 3 to 5 minutes. Toast the árbol chiles, turning them over and pressing down on them occasionally, until browned all over and with some blackened spots, about 8 minutes.

Grind or blend the chiles to a fine powder in a spice grinder or blender.

Makes ¼ cup.

....

TO SEED OR NOT TO SEED: Spiciness, from the tickle of a mole to the thrilling heat of a salsa, is essential to Mexican food. So when you cook with fresh and dried chiles employed for their heat as well as their flavor—for example, jalapeños and habaneros, chiles de árbol and chipotles—don't remove the seeds and veins, which contain a high concentration of capsaicin, the cause of that lovely burn. Larger, milder chiles, like poblanos, anchos, and guajillos, should be seeded and deveined.

☆ ☆

CHIPOTLES IN ADOBO: Nowadays this flavor-packed product is available in cans in most large supermarkets. Chipotles packed in a spiced puree make for a fiery, smoky ready-to-eat condiment. In recipes that call for chipotles in adobo, use the chiles themselves along with a little of the puree.

CILANTRO: Buy perky bright-green cilantro and, when you chop the herb, use the leaves and the stems. For the recipes in this book, finely chop cilantro, but there's no need to obsessively mince it.

Store cilantro, wrapped in a slightly damp paper towel and in a resealable bag with some air remaining inside, for up to five days in the fridge.

CREMA: Mexican crema is a fantastic thing—thick and rich but still decidedly drizzle-able. You can approximate its lovely texture and tang with a mixture of sour cream and crème fraîche lightly seasoned with salt.

EPAZOTE: Look for bunches of fresh epazote, which has an unforgettably pungent flavor, with perky, bright-green leaves; ignore the dried version.

Store epazote in the same way you would cilantro, but use it within three days.

LARD: The pale golden rendered pork fat (*manteca*, in Spanish) that you'll find in Mexican markets, not the snowy white lard you find most everywhere else, is what you want when you're making tamales. If you can't find it, swap it for the same amount of vegetable shortening.

Store lard for up to a few weeks in the fridge and a few months in the freezer.

LIMES: Limes with smooth, glossy skin are juicier than those with dull, slightly bumpy skin. Even these can vary in juice content, so always buy a few more than you think you'll need. If you're using the fruit's zest, be sure to wash the skin well.

Store limes in the fridge for up to a week.

MANGO: Buy the very best mangoes you can get your hands on. If you're lucky, that'll be a fragrant, creamy-fleshed ataulfo variety. If not, feel free to use the more common, larger, more fibrous Tommy Atkins mango. Ripe mangoes should give slightly when you squeeze them and should smell sweet and aromatic. You can also buy mangoes when they're firm and let them ripen at room temperature.

Store ripe mangoes in the fridge, where they'll keep for several days.

MASA: Fresh masa—starchy corn treated with calcium hydroxide (slaked lime) then ground into a dough—is wonderful but difficult to find in the U.S. So this book calls for the easy-to-find powdered dried masa called masa harina. Tamales and tortillas require a slightly different grind of masa harina, a coarser grind for the former than for the latter. The bag you buy should specify which of the two it's meant to make.

MEXICAN CHOCOLATE: Unlike the smooth, creamy product that Americans and Europeans are so fond of, Mexican chocolate contains crunchy grains of sugar and is spiked with cinnamon. Look for it in supermarkets (most common are the Ibarra and Abuelita brands), any Mexican market, and by mail order. If you must, substitute the same amount of semisweet chocolate.

MEXICAN CINNAMON: This fragrant spice—known as canela in Latin stores and elsewhere as Ceylon, Sri Lankan, or "true" cinnamon—comes mainly in delicate sticks. It is not the same as common cinnamon, which is stronger and spicier without canela's soft, almost vanilla-like aroma. Some recipes in this book call for ground Mexican cinnamon. Look for it in ground form or use a spice grinder to reduce sticks to a fine powder.

MEXICAN OREGANO: Dried Mexican oregano has a more floral, subtle flavor that the dried oregano you typically find at the supermarket. You may substitute regular dried oregano or marjoram, though always use a little less than the recipe calls for.

ONIONS: It deserves a reminder: When I call for white onions in this book, I mean those with white flesh and white skins, which you'll find at just about every supermarket. These onions have a slightly sweeter, crisper flesh and milder bite than yellow and Spanish onions, which are sometimes labeled as "white onions."

PICKLED JALAPEÑOS: These vinegar-soaked jalapeño chiles are a staple condiment, whether made in homes in Mexico or purchased in the cans readily available in the U.S. (For the right flavor, look for those whose ingredient list includes oil as well as vinegar.) They also make a great substitute for the typical cucumber pickle in non-Mexican recipes. When applying the strips of chile, make sure a little of the invigorating pickling liquid comes with them.

PILONCILLO: This unrefined sugar has a long history in Mexico and is worth seeking out for its complex flavor, though dark brown sugar makes an acceptable substitute. Often sold in solid, cone-shaped blocks, piloncillo must be grated or chopped in order to effectively measure it by volume for the recipes in this book.

SALT: Most recipes in this book call for kosher salt. You may use fine salt, but remember that you'll only need about 1 teaspoon fine salt for every 2 teaspoons kosher salt.

TAMARIND: This tart, tangy fruit comes in pale pods filled with sticky deep-brown pulp clinging to seeds or in packages containing just the pulp and seeds. Look for it in Asian and Latin markets, but do take care to avoid the "sweet" variety for the recipes in this book. Store it in the fridge for up to a few weeks.

TOMATILLOS: Crisp and tart when raw and pulpy and plum-like when cooked, this fantastic little fruit encased in a papery husk deserves your attention. Look for them in supermarkets and Latin markets, and choose tomatillos (pull back the husk and peek at the fruit) that are firm, free of bruises, and more or less free of wrinkles. When you're ready to use them, peel off the husks (choosing tomatillos with loose husks will make your life easier) and rinse them under cold water, rubbing with your fingers to remove the slightly sticky residue. Store them loose in the vegetable drawer for up to two weeks.

SOURCES

☆ ☆

FRIEDA'S

www.friedas.com

800-241-1771

Dried and fresh chiles, including poblanos and serranos, and other fresh ingredients, such as cactus pads, tamarind fruit, and plantains.

GOURMETSTORE.COM

www.gourmetstore.com

847-505-1021

Dried chiles such as chiles de árbol and guajillos (including powders and bulk orders), raw hulled pumpkin seeds, and ground Mexican cinnamon.

MELISSA GUERRA: TIENDA DE COCINA

www.melissaguerra.com

877-875-2665

Cooking equipment (cast-iron comales, molcajetes made from real volcanic stone, cast-aluminum tortilla presses, woven tortilla baskets) and pantry staples (corn husks for tamales, Mexican cinnamon, and piloncillo).

MELISSA'S

www.melissas.com

800-588-0151

Fresh ingredients, such as fresh habaneros, ataulfo mangoes, tomatillos, and banana leaves.

MEXGROCER.COM

www.mexgrocer.com

877-463-9476

Pantry ingredients like canned chipotles in adobo, pickled jalapeños, Mexican chocolate, dried masa, dried hoja santa leaves, dried hibiscus flowers, and corn husks.

PENZEYS SPICES

www.penzeys.com

800-741-7787

Spices, dried herbs, and dried chiles, such as ground and whole Mexican cinnamon, annatto seeds, Mexican oregano, and guajillo, chipotle mora, and ancho chiles.

RANCHO GORDO

www.ranchogordo.com

701-259-1935

Top-quality dried beans, piloncillo, Mexican oregano, Mexican cinnamon, and dried chiles de árbol.

INDEX

Page numbers in *italics* indicate illustrations.

☆ ☆

Salsa Verde Cruda, *132*, 133

L

Lamb Tacos, Slow-Cooked, 55
Lard, 208
Lemon Zest, Pico de Gallo with, 127
Licuado. *See* Smoothie
Lime, 208
    in Michelada, 173
    Pie, 184-185
    Pineapple, and Spinach Agua, 159
    Sorbet, 203
    -Strawberry Agua Fresca, *160*, 161
Limeade
    Mexican, 155
    Peanut, 162
Liver Tacos, Chopped, 51

M

Mango, 208
    -Apple Agua Fresca, 161
    Cream with Berries, *186*, 187
    Torito, 178
Mango-Apple Agua Fresca, 161
Margarita
    Cucumber-Ginger, 174
    Hibiscus, 174, *175*
    Pineapple, 176, *177*
    rimmed with salt, 175
Marinas
    with Mole, 86-87
    with Russian Salad, 88, *89*
Masa, 100, 208
    fresh, 11
    Tamale Dough, Basic, 104
Mezcal, 152
Michelada, 152, 173
Pineapple-Mint Sorbet, 202

Mole
    Chicken, 86
    Green (Pipián), Tortas with Chicken in,
        80-82, *81*
    Marinas with, 86-87
    Tamales with Chicken in, 102?
    Tortas de (variation), 87
Molletes, *64*, 65
Mortadella (Bologna) Torta, 66, *67*
Mushroom Tacos, 18, *19*

N

Nixtamal, 100
Nopales. *See* Cactus

O

Oatmeal, Orange, Carrot, and Papaya Smoothie
    with, 166
Olive(s)
    Ground Beef, and Raisin Tacos (Picadillo),
        52, 53-54
    in Tamales from Chiapas, 106-108, *107*
Onions
    Pickled, Guadalajara-Style, 147
    Pickled, Red, 147
    white, 209
Orange, Carrot, and Papaya Smoothie with
    Oatmeal, 166
Oregano, Mexican, 209

P

Pachola Burgers, 94-96, *95*
Papalo, in Cemitas, 93
Papaya, Orange, and Carrot Smoothie with
    Oatmeal, 166
Pasilla Chile Garnish, Crispy, 36
Peanut
    Limeade, 162
    Torito, 178, *179*

☆ ☆